AF316640

Finding Your Way Back Home

Sean Austin

Dedication

First and foremost, I would like to dedicate this book to God!!! Thank you for the many signs to write this book!!! Secondly, to my Mother and Father for your unconditional love and support since day 1.

Acknowledgment

I would like to acknowledge Pacific Ghostwriting for their professionalism and help in bringing this book to life. Specifically, James Sullivan, without you reaching out to me, the book may not have been completed.

About the Author

Sean Austin resides in Canada and continues to help people achieve their fitness goals to this day. My goal when deciding to write this book was to help a person to even help 1 person realize there is always hope and to be the best you can be.

Sean is a competitive bodybuilder, a loving husband, and a caring father to one son and numerous fur babies. Sean is looking forward to working on a second book upcoming in the near future!

Preface

This book gives an insight into my journey in this life. You will embark on my expedition of resilience, redemption, and unwavering faith. It talks about how my life descended into darkness as a result of drug addiction. As I battled the demons inside me and dealt with the fallout from my decisions, my path was paved with heartache, loss, and despair.

But amidst the chaos and turmoil, I discovered a glimmer of hope—a beacon of light that guided me through the darkest of nights. Through the depths of my struggles, I found solace and strength in my newfound faith in God.

As you delve into my story, you will witness the raw and unfiltered truth of addiction's grip and the devastating toll it takes on those we hold dear. Along with that, you will also witness the transformative power of faith and the miraculous journey of recovery that unfolds when one man surrenders his life to God's grace.

Prepare to be moved, inspired, and uplifted as you follow my voyage from the depths of desolation to the pinnacle of divine grace. My story serves as a testament to the indomitable spirit of the human soul and the boundless mercy of a loving God.

Contents

Chapter 1: Early Childhood

The beauty of life lies in its unpredictability. I have always believed in living life to the fullest, always being at the edge, and never backing down from a challenge. I always set dreams and goals so high without wondering about the consequences. Maybe it was my hunger to be successful or retaliation against the boredom of my life. Still, whatever I did in life, from becoming a competitive bodybuilder to being arrested in a drug case, I did it with freedom and confidence.

You might have heard the phrase, *"Life is like a box of chocolate with many flavors, shapes, and sizes."* Well, I believe life is meant to be lived, enjoyed, and acknowledged. Your priorities and goals should hold meaning; they should be welcoming to new experiences. They should allow you to spread your wings outside your comfort zone. My journey has been somewhat like that, as experimenting with life and its choices was my favorite hobby.

I was born in Delta, British Columbia, Canada, into a beautiful, loving, and caring household. I had great parents and a partially awesome but somewhat troubled older brother. My grandmother also lived with us in the basement. My father, Jack Austin, was a hard-working man with moral and family values. He started his profession as a teacher, and with time, dedication, and honesty, he became the principal and, eventually, superintendent of the school district. From him, the love for education and learning descended into our entire family. He was a good, disciplined, yet modern dad. Even though my brother was a tough lad and listening to his complaints every day was a hectic job, he took care of him incredibly. He never judged us on our past decisions and always guided us for the future. His guidance was like a runway where we took off toward life with all its success.

My mother, Samantha Austin, worked as a secretary in schools as well as for an insurance company. She was incredible at both work and home. She was a devoted mother who found a sound balance between work, motherhood, family, and self-care. There is nothing purer than a mother's love, and my mother has always showered our entire family with her love and care, and that has enabled us to achieve more in life. She was a tremendous role model and a symbol of prosperity growing up. Because I was somewhat of an introvert, I was always quiet and kept to myself, but my mother somehow always knew what I wanted to say. She understood my needs better than I did. The sacrifices she made in her life and the countless nights she spent worrying for us hold a special place in my heart.

My parents were totally in love with each other. They showed us what it truly meant to be in love. I don't think the younger generation understands the power of love, nor do they feel the true nature of love beyond physical touch. I saw my father defending my mother when she was not around and saw my mother taking care of my father's needs without him even asking. They respected each other and balanced their marriage oh so perfectly. From them, I learned how important it is for a couple to achieve and develop understanding between each other. A spouse is like the other half of a body with the same heart. My parents were a remarkable duo with one mind, heart, and soul. Maybe it was my naivety or the fact that failed marriages have become so common in society, but I always saw my parents as a perfect couple and still do to this day.

I grew up in a Christian family, and although we believed in God, we weren't a very religious or conservative family. My parents believed in God but did not force us to go to church or read the Bible. Instead, they wanted us to develop our relationship with religion on our own accord. They believed that force wasn't needed to create attraction toward religion. Instead, people should be drawn by its beauty.

My Nana was the most religious and pious person in the household. You could expect her to know many verses by heart from the Bible. She used to visit the church every Sunday and always preached to us. I was close to my Nana, also known as Grandma Margot. Maybe that is why some of her religious traits were passed down to me through her.

I remember I used to pray a lot and have a conversation with God about my issues and personal problems, and all of these acts were driven by myself. They were not advised or purposely imposed on me. I did them with pure intentions. I was driven toward the concept of religion because I refused to believe that this world was a meaningless place. I refused to believe that there were no consequences to our actions in the hereafter despite God drawing a clear line between the good and the evil in this life.

The thought that every action we performed in this world could be unaccountable and go unanswered terrified me. I could not believe in such an ideology. I always felt relief when I prayed or talked to God. Prayers felt like protection from my dad and the love of my mother. They felt like the wisdom of my Nana and the courage of my brother. All those things elevated me to new heights. I saw all this hopelessness among my friends and even some family members, and I always advised them to trust God and His plan. I have never backed down from saying what I feel like, whether it's about religion or something else.

My Nana was the nicest person I have ever met. She was like a second mother to my brother and me. Whenever my parents were busy with work, they would leave us under Nana's care. She was more than just a grandmother. She was my first true friend. She is the one who taught us many moral values and work ethics.

With all these incredibly loving and kind people in my life, there was someone else, too. While I was always considered the "good kid," my older brother Keith was a wild and devilish child. As kids, we had a good relationship. We played with toys and watched movies together. However, as we grew up, I saw him always getting in trouble and running for his life. He was a rebellious kid who did not like authority. I remember seeing him bullying my friends in front of me and teasing them for no good reason. He didn't do anything cruel but was mean to many people, including me. The two of us were like different sides of the same coin. While we were related by blood, our personalities were poles apart. I played by the rules; he always broke them. He would get into trouble at school, while I would listen to the teachers and usually stay low.

My brother was an extrovert. He had lots of friends and loved to be the center of attention all the time. He loved teasing and pranking others, so he was considered a fun kid. On the other hand, I was shy. I loved to be left alone with my toys and my books or thoughts as I grew up. I was a quick learner, so naturally, I was a good student who secured high grades. Unlike my brother, I was the favorite of my teachers, neighbors, and maybe even my family. My brother always got scolded because of his childish mischief while I felt connected to my emotions and mind. However, the one thing that I shared with my brother, the only common ground we had growing up, was our love for sports. We were both crazy when it came to it.

I started playing different sports like baseball, basketball, and soccer at an early age. I was really good back then. However, my performance declined after I stopped giving them attention and value. I was a high-performance kid with an excellent position in class and sports. My brother, however, loved playing and watching football. It suited his personality, too. He was strong, ruthless, brave, and arrogant, like any NFL player. He used to play in a team that my dad managed. Before my brother started getting into trouble frequently and my father started getting annoyed by him being around, they both loved spending time together and learning from each other. Even though my father's career progressed from his teaching days, he still made sure that he never retired from learning or imparting knowledge. My father's hunger for education and learning a new skill was never satisfied.

My brother was two years older than me, and according to him, those were the best two years of his life. Of course, as an elder brother, he teased me a lot, but he helped me a lot, too. From childhood, I have been looking up to him; however, I believe he has taught me more indirectly than directly. My love for sports also comes indirectly through him; at some point in my childhood, maybe his toys introduced me to these beautiful sports.

I'm sure my brother must have protected me from things without even mentioning it. Even though I had no doubt he could trade me off for a new video game, deep down in his heart, I knew he loved me.

I started playing soccer when I was five years old, and I remember one instance when I was playing soccer and injured myself badly. I was so much in pain that I cried and screamed, but my brother and his friends thought I was making a scene and only doing it for attention. In their defense, I do admit that I wasn't the best player and would often cry wolf for nothing, so I guess they couldn't tell that I was really hurt this time around. I was crying in pain but was left on the field. After the game, our parents came to pick us up and saw my "injury." The pain had become unbearable at this point. I was holding my arm, and tears filled my eyes. Finally, after a day of agonizing pain, my Nana took me to the hospital, where the doctor took an X-ray of my arm, and it was as I had expected —I had broken my arm. My parents felt really bad about that.

One of my fondest memories from my childhood is our family reunions. My brother and I loved holidays, especially the time of the year when the whole family would gather under one roof. We got to spend quality time with our cousins and friends.

I loved all the family reunions because they used to be so much fun, but the family BBQs held a special place. It is ironic how the celebration of the same event can be so different a few years apart. As kids, Halloween used to mean costumes and candy, and Christmas used to be all about gifts and cookies, but everything changed with time, I guess. As I grew older, I got more party invitations than I could count for family gatherings, but I preferred spending my time elsewhere.

Childhood is like a rollercoaster ride; while we are on it, rather than enjoying the ride, we waste it screaming. I always see my childhood as a beautiful chapter of my life, with great people lifting me and raising me to my full potential. That time of my life was full of joy and sorrow, excitement and boredom. Every emotion tells a different tale, but putting them together made me the kind of person I am today. Everything from my childhood holds a special place in my heart when I look back. From dressing up for Halloween with my brother to playing with cousins, crying over stupid things, and receiving unconditional love from everyone, all these memories help put a smile on my face, especially when I need it the most.

I had a great childhood with so many people to look up to and learn from; it was undoubtedly a privilege to be born into such a loving household. I wished I had the same technological advancement available when I was a child. All these incidents are held close to my heart, but unfortunately, I don't have many pictures of those moments, so I can only reminisce about those times by relying on my memory. The memories that stayed with me from my childhood, the age of innocence, are among the greatest treasures I possess. My childhood was undoubtedly great, but no one could have prepared me for what was to come in the near future.

Chapter 2: Junior High

Junior High was an emotional roller coaster ride. It was a platform for me to learn and grow my personal and social skills. As I had a shy and conserved personality, adjusting to a new place was not easy for me. Just the thought of joining junior high would make me nervous. I had always been like this, and even before my first day, I was super nervous. As an introvert, I was usually not a big fan of change. I liked things as they were, especially when they went according to my plan. People would assume I was boring, but I liked things unchanged until necessary. So, when I graduated from elementary school, I knew the day would come when I would eventually enter junior high. Still, just because I knew it would happen didn't make it better.

My parents always supported me and protected me at every step, but school in Canada can be challenging for many people. Junior high can be traumatic for students as they face bullies and verbal abuse at such a young age. In a country like Canada, it is natural for you to be afraid of school as all the bullying and beating that children go through is a reality and can leave you traumatized for the rest of your life. Many children have a fear of joining school because of such reasons. In my case, I got really lucky as I had a big brother. I enrolled at Junior Secondary School. My brother was already studying there, and he was in grade 10 when I arrived. Our relationship as brothers may have been a bumpy road, but I knew I could always count on him to have my back, and his presence made me feel secure.

Junior Secondary School was much bigger than I had anticipated. I remember feeling anxious that I would be late for my first class as the school was significantly bigger than my elementary school or my imagination. In the beginning, I would get lost searching for my classroom, as all the routes were new to me. However, I met many new people and made new friends. Once I settled down, things became routine, and I even became a little famous, if I do say so myself. I broke out of my shell and made a name for myself. I started playing sports and hanging out with my new friends over the weekend. My school had many sports programs and hosted several events throughout the year. Sports was the most familiar area for me, and it helped me adjust better in school. It helped me create new and strong friendships. Being good at sports improved my image among my classmates and other students. I wasn't a one-sport kind of a kid, either. I loved exploring every sport I came across.

My brother protected me from a group of boys who would harass me when I walked to school back in eighth grade. They always wanted to see what I had in my lunch and just loved bugging me in general. They were a year older than me, and they thought I was an easy target. I was tired of their harassment, but I felt embarrassed asking Keith for help because I thought I should be able to face them myself. However, as the bullying became intolerable, I became so paranoid that walking up the street would leave me in a panic. When it got to that point, I asked my brother if he would walk to school with me one day.

As we walked up the hill, I remember thinking to myself, *"Oh boy, here we go!"* As we were walking, the main bully approached us. My brother walked right up to him, tossed him to the ground, and said, "From now on, there are not going to be any more issues here. *Are there?"* My brother had plenty of savage moments in his life, from smoking weed in his car just before school started to buying his younger brother and his friend beer, but this, right here, I swear it looked more badass than it sounds. It was a clear message to every bully on the block or school about who the real boss was. Let's just say no one ever bothered me after that. Having the toughest kid in school, as your brother did, has its perks, after all. At that moment, I was really proud to have my brother by my side.

My popularity began to grow in school and outside. I enjoyed the attention, but I never wanted it to be at the expense of someone else. I liked people respecting and loving me, but I didn't particularly appreciate making fun of someone's pain or nervousness.

In terms of academics, I was beloved by my teachers. I was good at studying, averaging a B, and my sense of humor always made the teacher and the class laugh. I was an easy-going student, never cared too much, and was always in a light mood. I loved this new side of mine, more involved and more invested in the world around me. I even did some things during junior high that I would never have thought of.

I threw my first house party with a couple of friends. I remember I found out my parents and my brother were not going to be home one particular night. My parents were gone for the entire night, but my brother was supposed to be back in a few hours. I didn't expect him to come back anytime soon, so I sent invitations for the party.

I remember when the first person showed up, my Nana came out from her side of the house and asked me who it was. "This is

Dildo, Nana," I told her, trying to hold my laughter. My Nana, God bless her heart, greeted him with, "Hello, Dildo." After she retreated back to the basement, people started arriving one by one. In total, I think around 50 people showed up at the party.

The party was terrific, and the kids really enjoyed it, but then I realized why kids are not allowed to throw parties like that. Things started to get a little out of hand, and the partygoers became hard to manage. I could hear sounds from things falling and shattering into pieces in the house. Some of the kids were entering my parents' and brother's room, wreaking havoc, and that was crossing the line. I was trying to control and manage the party as I was having a great time as well and didn't want to end it, but it needed to be shut down instantly.

When my brother came home, he saw all these children partying, dancing, and running all over the house. It made him so mad he started to scream, "Get out of the house now!!" I had to sensor some words as my brother was a hothead. He ran after my friends, and the sight of him screaming at them was scarier than the Grim Reaper. Kids started to run outside the house. As I have mentioned before, my brother had quite the reputation for being the toughest bully on the block. Some kids recognized him and ran instantly, and the rest fled our home after hearing his threats. My parents were not impressed in the least when they returned home, and of course, I got punished for my shenanigans. I was grounded for the next two weeks.

During junior high, I became more social and extroverted. Maybe the right crowd enabled me and helped me come out of my comfort zone. My shyness slowly turned into confidence. I had a good group of friends who played sports together, whether it was basketball, volleyball, or football. Our love for sports brought us together and created a special bond between us. I had many friends, but the one I was closest to was Drew. We were like two peas in a pod. He and I always hung out together, doing the typical thing young boys did. We played video games and sports, and he was the first person I ever got drunk with. There was another lifelong friend, Brian. He lives in California now, and we have known each other since we were 4. We played sports together back then and were close. We are still close to this day and try to meet each other whenever possible.

There are some bonds thicker than blood, and these were the ones I created in junior high. I made some great friends who helped me laugh in the most challenging times. They supported me through my years in junior high and beyond. This bond was created through sports, and everyone always admired it. Friends like these are true gems. You don't get to see them every day. As life progresses, responsibilities can drag them away, but you know they will always be there for you if you need them. All memories are cherished and remembered with the purest intentions. They are like your brothers. They won't admit their love for you but will always silently protect you. I am glad to say I met some of the greatest selfless people during junior high.

Usually, people are afraid of their older brothers. They don't want to get caught drinking or smoking by them, but that did not happen in my case. I don't know if I should call my brother the most astonishing or the dumbest person alive because I smoked weed with him for the first time in grade 8.

My brother had recently attained his driver's license, and my parents had given him their old green Maverick to drive to school.

With a reckless history like his, you wouldn't expect him to do anything wise. As we drove to school, he decided it was a good idea to turn the car into a hotbox before we turned up to school. For those who don't know what a hotbox is, it's when you lock your car airtight and smoke weed inside, trapping all the smoke in. Not going to lie; it looked cool, but with underage kids, it is not a wise idea, especially right before school. Blaming everything on Keith would be a little unjust because deep down inside, I wanted to know what smoking weed felt like, too.

At this point in my life, I did whatever my brother wanted me to do and decided to go with it. Thanks to my brother, I was living the dream of every shy junior high student – I was safe from bullies. I was just a kid getting high with his brother back then, but I was not good at hiding or managing it at all. I nearly got caught by many of my teachers. I remember feeling foggy coming out of the car after smoking weed and having to go to a cooking class. I was a few minutes late, and I remember when I walked in, everyone was staring at me. I sat in my seat at a group table and was very incoherent. I could not understand anything that the teacher was saying. My classmates laughed at me, teasing me about how red my eyes were. Being high has some funny drawbacks as well. The memory of some incidents can be different from what actually happened, but it was a fun day from what I remember. That was the first and last time I smoked weed before school.

During junior high, I was really living like a king. My next achievement was to try alcohol. I first drank alcohol in grade 8 with my friend Drew. When we planned on trying alcohol for the first time, we were presented with the issue of how to get our hands on it. The first person that came to my mind was my brother and he was the one who ended up getting us beer. I still remember how it felt, the first sip and its smell. I even remember its name, "Lucky Beer." After we drank it, though, I did not feel so lucky. Our heads started spinning, and we passed out on a pull-out couch in my parents' basement. Maybe the lucky part was that my parents were not present at home that day. We were woken up by the great Keith Austin, who had come home and thought it would be funny to wake us up by hitting us with a bamboo stick. I jumped out in my sleep while my brother proceeded to roll Drew up in the bed and attempt to close it. We couldn't really make sense of the situation at the time but had a good, hard laugh when we thought about it the next day.

When I look back, I realize I will always be in debt to my brother, as he has given me such unforgettable and beautiful memories. Without him, I might have never dared to live so freely. After so many years, even remembering it now puts a smile on my face. Maybe that is what life is about, "living every moment and making every second count."

I had been on the school sports teams since eighth grade. After the basketball season in grade 8, I was chosen to attend camp for the top and most improved players in the province with the best coaches. I was very nervous, but it was an honor to have been chosen for such an event. It was a great experience – I had fun and learned a lot.

I was one of the best players on the grade 8 team, so imagine my surprise when the basketball season came around in grade 9, and I was cut by the coach. I was shocked I didn't make the team. So, instead of practicing and getting better for when grade 10 came around, I just gave up and didn't bother trying out for the team again. That is something I regret to this day. I can't help but think, *"What if? What if I had tried a little harder?"* Maybe I'm not the only one who thinks like that in life. But we have to live with our decisions and their consequences.

During these years, my brother was heavily invested in bodybuilding and working out. He was spending more and more time in the gym, and no doubt, it was paying off. My brother's physical health improved insanely. He was always a strong and rough guy, but now, he looked like a force to be reckoned with. He introduced me to the gym in the most bizarre way possible. He told me I was not good enough to become a bodybuilder, and being his brother, how could I walk away from a challenge like that? In grade 9, I started working out. I was furious. How could he or anyone else underestimate me? I started hitting the gym; not only did I want to get in shape, but I also wanted to get into professional bodybuilding and participate in a competition to prove him wrong.

During junior high, I remember having a horrible case of the flu. I fell sick and was fighting for my life. Okay, I may be exaggerating, but it really felt that way. My parents, being the kind souls they were, were so worried about me that they bought me the original Nintendo system that I badly wanted to cheer me up.

Grade 10 was a complete blast. I used to attend parties, smoke weed, and drink beer with friends, and I even tried acid for the first time. I want to tell you how it felt, but all I can remember is a blackout and waking up the next morning with a spinning head. Grade 10 is when I became obsessed with working out and wanted my body to get in shape. Like every young man, I tried to look insanely good. I tried to work on my body and make it look handcrafted by God. I loved working out and going to the gym. My training at the gym was also helping me perform better in sports. My football team won the provincial championships. After my friend Drew got injured, we got into a bad situation. He was our best player, and we rallied behind him. Every player came through with the performance of a lifetime that day. I was so proud to be on a team of such excellent players and performers.

In terms of my dating life, although I did have some girlfriends on and off during junior high, I dated my first serious girlfriend in grade 10, and we lasted for the entirety of that year. I remember being at my girlfriend's house, and we were about to have sex for the first time. We thought she wasn't home, but she returned early that day, and walking past the room, she slammed the door. Her mom was furious, especially with the fact that I was naked in bed. She told my girlfriend if she ever saw my bare butt again in her house, it was getting a whooping. Now, I can laugh at this incident, but it felt like a genuine threat back then.

Besides the crazy things I did in junior high, it is also memorable for many other great moments. For instance, I remember I got selected after auditioning for a role in a school play in grade 10. It was a play called Isabella, which is about a girl who joins the guys' football team. I was selected as the school jock and bully who did not want her on the team. It was a fun experience, and I discovered that day that I loved performing in front of an audience.

Grade 10 was full of fun and new experiences, but it was also the time I experienced one of the saddest moments of my life. It was when our beloved family dog Whiskey passed away. I remember my parents and brother were away that day, and I was home alone with Nana. Whiskey passed away, and I had to bring him to the vet all by myself.

I was roughly eight years old when my folks adopted Whiskey. I walked into the backyard one day, and this white fluff ball came running at me. From then on, he became part of the family, and we all loved him. He was especially close to my mom. Sometimes, Whiskey would get annoyed with my brother and me when we played super dog and flew him across our bed, holding him up, and then crashed and landed into the bed. He would always try and run out of the room.

Whiskey's passing was very emotional for me. We all had a special bond with him, so acknowledging his death was a challenging moment in our lives, especially mine, as I had to go through it all alone. Still, I think it helped me deal with the loss of a loved one.

When I look back on those junior high years, I think it was a transition period of my life in becoming a man. Before starting junior high, I was a naive and shy kid. Junior high helped me develop many skills and bonds that I never knew I would love so much. It helped me improve my athletic skills. It showed me new sides of my brother, from being my weed and alcohol carrier to my biggest protective shield. I looked up to my brother and admired his courage to face every threat and problem head-on. He was my inspiration growing up. The first time I ever went to the gym and worked out was because of my brother.

Chapter 3: High School

Unlike Junior High, my High School years were a smooth ride. I attended the North Delta Senior Secondary High School, and since Junior High had helped me come out of my shell, I did not have to work on my social skills further. Instead, I was focused on playing football, smoking weed, drinking beer, and being a heartbreaker. Despite being a fun person, I paid attention to the lectures during class and secured satisfactory grades, always B's and C's. At that point, I was mature enough to differentiate between when I was supposed to have fun and when I had to study. My teachers liked me for that reason and, of course, my fantastic sense of humor.

The only trouble I had with my studies in high school was in 11th-grade chemistry class with Mr. Appleton. I struggled a lot with his class, mainly because of his teaching style. It was hard to learn from, and with chemistry being my weak point, this class became a nightmare for me. But that wasn't all. The most unfortunate incident occurred when he caught me cheating on an exam. I was trying to copy the answers from my classmate's paper when he glanced over and caught me red-handed. It was so evident that I felt ashamed. He took away my answer sheet, and thoughts about scoring a 0 and failing the class clouded my mind. Finally, I lost my composure and started screaming at him about being falsely accused. In my distress, he returned my answer sheet, threatening that he would grade my paper with an F if I cheated again.

My relationship with my brother was quite close at this point. As I have mentioned before, he was the reason my interest in bodybuilding developed. Back when I was in junior high, Keith started working on making his body look better and more attractive. In the midst of it, he somehow managed to gain my interest in this activity by mocking me, saying that I could never be better at bodybuilding than him. His arrogant behavior made me more furious with each passing day. And so, toward the end of Junior High, I started working out. I could not stand the thought of someone, especially my brother, underestimating me. Not only did I start bodybuilding to get in shape, but I also decided to adopt the same as a profession and participate in competitions solely to prove my brother wrong.

However, as time went on, my passion for proving my brother wrong faded. I worked out due to my interest in building muscles and becoming strong. However, I still looked up to my brother as a role model because of his lean figure and toned muscles.

The summer after my brother graduated from high school, I was invited to a house party. I was starting grade 11 at this point. There must have been around 100 kids in attendance at that party, and the majority of them were around my brother's age, who had just graduated. I remember being nervous at first, as I was among a crowd of people a few years older than me. At that stage, it stresses many people, and I felt no different. But being a 6ft. tall fellow, weighing around 210 lbs., I immediately regained my confidence, thinking I could handle a fight if one were to occur. That was when I encountered Ben. Ben had also recently graduated and was extremely drunk when he started arguing with me. I was wearing my brother's Gold's Gym sweater (that he loved!) for the party, and when Ben approached me, he tore the sweater apart. Right that second, I saw Ben from a distance.

He was a friend of my brother's, and upon seeing what had just happened, he approached us, mouthing the words "Finish him" to me as he did. Ben and I tussled around and blew a few punches at Ben, and he fought back. Unfortunately, it resulted in a tie, with neither side incurring too much damage. As we were leaving the party, I remember yelling at Ben that he had just ruined my brother's favorite shirt and he was going to regret it. After a few days, my brother confronted Ben and told him to pay back for the sweater. Being sober then and admitting his mistake, Ben agreed and paid my brother the exact money he demanded.

My brother worked various odd jobs after graduating from high school, such as selling vacuums, serving as a waiter, etc. However, by the time he turned 19, he had settled in quite nicely as a bill collector and moved to Toronto to work for a collection agency there. I was 17 when he moved away, but he would often come to North Delta to visit us. Life felt different whenever my brother was home, as we frequently got into fights, and it was kind of weird not having him around for the rest of the year.

As my brother had moved to Toronto, I was mostly on my own. I realized that I had come a long way when I bravely faced situations where neither my brother nor his friends were there to help me. That phase of my life began at a house party in the 12th grade. It was the weekend, and with so many kids at this party, some fights were bound to break out. Out on the street, I was in the middle of a fight, and an unknown guy started interfering. Annoyed, I pushed him down when, all of a sudden, his girlfriend jumped on my back and started scratching me. Watching closely, a friend of mine decided to help in a way that could have killed me later on. He grabbed the guy's girlfriend and threw her on the ground. The girl thought that it was me who had tossed her and left, yelling that I would reap what I had sown. On the other hand, I paid no heed to her words and continued fighting.

The weekend passed, and on Monday, another fight was set up in the parking lot of Sunscape Arena. It was the continuation of a fight that had broken out between two guys at the party. Hundreds of young kids turned up in the parking lot on Monday, and the two fellows started to throw punches at each other at once. The fight had just started, and all eyes were fixed on the two young men. Then, all of a sudden, a roar of motorcycles could be heard approaching. As two bikes and a vintage Chevrolet El Camino appeared in the parking lot, the crowd turned toward them in confusion. Four enormous guys with tattoos all over their bodies stepped out of the vehicle. They were all wearing sunglasses, and it seemed as if one of them had a pistol. From the looks of it, they were gangsters, gangsters who were making their way through the crowd asking, "Who is Sean Austin?"

As every finger pointed toward me, the sea parted, and every soul moved to the side while the group made their way up to me.

"I heard you hurt my niece," the biggest of the bunch said. At that moment, it was clear to me that I was in trouble.

"Sorry, sir. I did not do anything to her. It was a misunderstanding," I replied and explained what had happened that night.

I thanked my lucky stars that they actually bought it. But they didn't leave without warning.

"Alright, but if I hear anything about you coming near her or harming her from now on, you will be seeing me again," he warned me as I gulped and replied, "That will not happen again, sir. And thank you for believing me."

After that, they walked away as I stood there, amazed at my act of courage. Instead of running away in fright, I could not believe that I faced this gigantic bearded gangster.

A few years later, I ran into the same girl from that party, and she recognized me at once. She apologized to me for what she had done all those years ago. Surprised, I laughed as I recalled the whole event and assured her that we were young and that it was all water under the bridge now. I still remember the incident to this day, and it serves as a pleasant memory from my teenage years.

The boost of confidence that I got in high school was thanks to my brother. He was pretty supportive of my enthusiasm for football and loved it when I did well. His way of supporting me was by attending all my games and encouraging me to celebrate every time I performed well. After he moved, my parents took on that role.

My brother had a major influence on my life, sometimes positive and sometimes negative, but being a teenager, he often put me in the most embarrassing situations. One of those situations was when Keith, my friend Harry, and I went to the premiere of Jurassic Park. We were in the parking lot, standing in a long queue to get into the local cinema. I was walking ahead of my brother and Harry when the lane moved, and to my surprise, Harry suddenly pulled down my shorts. I was in shock as I miserably tried to pull them back up. Right then, my brother stepped on my underwear and pushed me over. I fell to the ground in front of hundreds of people and lay naked, struggling to pull my shorts and underwear up. With hundreds of people laughing at me, one could see the embarrassment on my face as I stood back up again after somehow managing to pull my shorts up. It is one of those memories that are fun to look back on but were definitely not amusing when they happened.

Life with friends and football might have been great in high school, but nothing major happened when it came to my love life. My girlfriend from junior high broke up with me and started dating an older guy. It may sound like a cliché now, but it was my first experience with a broken heart back then. My brother had moved to Toronto by then, so I had my mother console me. But it hurt me so much that I did not have a proper relationship afterward for the next two years in high school. Only once did I date a girl, but that lasted for a month as I got bored and moved on. Being a jock, I was pretty popular, so I slept with as many girls as possible without getting into a relationship. One could say that I had become a teenage womanizer!

However, my fate of finding myself in embarrassing situations followed me into my love life. I remember attending a party with a bunch of unknown girls around. I was excited as I thought that I might be able to meet someone new there. But my chances went to zero when I started playing the drinking games around the coffee table and lost. As a result, I had to drink a tremendous amount of beer. I accepted my defeat and kept chugging the beer until I could taste the Chinese food I had eaten earlier. That was my moment of "Oh, no!" and without skipping another beat, I puked all over the girls at the coffee table. My chances of taking a girl home turned negative, and the host of the party also looked pretty annoyed with me. So, with my tail between my legs, I called a cab and went straight home. That night is not only a striking memory but also a lesson learned, that is, always have good intentions!

High school is the most rebellious part of people's lives, and they often look back at it, realizing how carefree they were. Whether it is about being overly sexual or getting in trouble, all kinds of weird risks are taken. In the same way, drugs are also newly introduced to kids at this age, but that was not the case for me. I often smoked weed with my brother in Junior High, but other drugs did not arouse my curiosity. Weed was the only thing I smoked during most of my high school years.

After my brother's graduation party, a friend of his stayed at our house. My brother and his friend were in his room when I walked in and saw them sniffing cocaine. His friend panicked, thinking I would tell my parents, but I never planned to do that. Being the cool but reckless brother that he was, he offered me to try it. I declined. At this time, I had just started 12th grade and did not think much of it as I did not want to try anything else except weed.

It was not until my high school graduation party that I tried cocaine and acid for the first time. My graduation was relatively uneventful. My friends and I had a small party, drank, and drove around in a limo for a while before heading to my friend's house to spend the night. We were the only ones in his house as his parents were away. So, around five guys, including me, did cocaine for the first time that night. To this day, that night is a blur to me. I can only recall staying awake till quite late in the morning because we could not sleep.

Overall, I was a carefree kid till high school and never thought much about my future. I focused on living in the moment and making the most out of it. Therefore, my high school years were spent having fun with my friends and playing football. But those two years passed by in a flash, and suddenly, it was graduation day. I saw people leaving for college, and my friends started talking about career goals and plans. And I realized that I had not decided what I wanted to do with my life yet. So I ruined my graduation with the constant thought of "What will I do with myself now?" I thought this the whole time, whether during the parties or while drinking and driving around in a limousine with my friends.

High School might have been the last point in my life where I was truly carefree. And that is what makes it the most memorable of times since I enjoyed my life to my heart's desire till the end.

Chapter 4: Struggles of a Teenager

The core purpose of high school might be attaining education, but for me, it was everything except that. Even though I was an average enough student, most of my time in high school was spent playing football, attending parties with my friends, and getting in fights. I had the most memorable time with my friends back then and enjoyed every second of it.

However, I couldn't be my usual carefree and somewhat careless self my whole life, and that realization dawned heavily on me after I graduated high school. Realizing I had no plans for my future, I started exploring career options and gaining some knowledge about the career fields that would suit me best. That is when I thought of how proud I had always been of my father, who made his way up from a teacher to a principal and now served as the superintendent of the school district. I realized that he had climbed the ladder from being a regular teacher to achieving one of the highest ranks in the administration of the education system through dedication and hard work. At that moment, I realized how close my source of inspiration was, but I had been searching for it in the wrong places. So, I decided to join college, hoping to follow in my father's footsteps to become a teacher like him someday and make him proud.

With a determined heart and a keen spirit, I finally made a move and applied for admission to the Kwantlen Polytechnic University (KPU) in Surrey, British Colombia. Luckily, I got in and selected history as my major. I set my mind to studying as much as possible because I knew that if I failed to get my degree and succeed as a teacher, I did not have a backup plan. And not having a backup plan meant I had to finish my degree against all odds.

Studying in college was very different from high school, but I made a great start because of my steady perseverance. The university environment was also the opposite of my high school because most college students were committed to their degrees and future goals, which was a new experience for me. While it's not to say that I didn't take my education seriously and did not put my blood, sweat, and tears into my degree, I couldn't change my personality overnight. I still needed something to let off steam, like playing some sport, hitting the gym, or just hanging out with my old friends, and because of that, I sometimes fell behind in half of my class.

However, the main reason my college life was poles apart from my high school life was that I rarely hung out with people at college and did not have many friends either. My high school life was all about spending time with friends and partying. Therefore, the sudden lifestyle change felt harsh, but I got used to it with time. Another reason was that even though people were serious about their studies and goals, they were surrounded by people of the same nature, people who shared the same interests. But that was not the case with me. I could not meet many people with the same interests as me, so my usual routine in college consisted of taking classes and simply going home or to the gym. As a result, I also do not possess any delightful memories of that time in my life, except for when I went to a strip club with another classmate, and we watched strippers while drinking beer together. Other than that, my college life was quite uneventful.

While the 19-year-old me managed my college studies on one side, I also worked as the manager of a Blockbuster. So, life was hectic, and I barely had the energy to take time out for extra studies. Besides working at the Blockbuster store, I worked multiple other odd jobs as a teenager. For example, after grade 12, I worked as a deckhand at the Harbor City Patrol during the summer. I also worked as a tower guard at the waterslide park named Splashdown Waterpark. Other than that, I served as a delivery driver for a Chinese food restaurant. And also worked in the construction field in my friend's dad's construction company for some time.

As time passed, I became heavily invested in bodybuilding, so I didn't pay attention to my studies because most of my time was spent at the gym or at work. There were times when I got so hyped up about going to the gym that I even missed my classes every once in a while, simply because I loved passing my time inside the gym corridors, working to build my muscles.

Despite working all these odd jobs and earning some extra income, I was living paycheck to paycheck during my college life. Because of my expensive habit of living to become a bodybuilder, most of my money was spent on my diet. At this point in my life, when I was too short of money, I decided to start stripping at ladies' nightclubs so I could make a few extra dollars. But it was a tiring routine: attending classes, stripping in the evening, and doing a vigorous workout all the time.

One day, a fellow bodybuilder told me about how he was making good money from stripping. After 15 minutes of work, he would walk away with $150! For someone working multiple jobs to stay afloat, it sounded like the dream job. The thought was also compelling because it was a source of validation for my body. Since I was heavier throughout my teenage years, I always got bullied by my brother in different ways, such as being called an egg on a daily basis. That made me feel insecure and pushed me harder to build muscle and lose weight. Therefore, I felt thrilled once I got into shape, and now I had a chance to truly show off. At first, I was a little shy and nervous about going on stage, but I got used to it after a while. It also helped me gain confidence because of the attention I got from all the ladies while stripping.

During that time, my brother moved back from Toronto to North Delta. Since the company he worked for had a better opportunity for him back home, he managed to get a transfer and return home.

When my brother first moved to Toronto, I was genuinely happy that he had finally found a well-paying job. But I always knew that one way or another, he would return home someday. But despite that, my feelings and emotions upon his arrival home were extraordinary, as I had missed him a lot without even realizing it.

Upon going down memory lane, a hilarious incident pops up in my head when I think about my college times. It was when I worked at a bar called Chicago's as a stripper. So before going to strip, my brother and one of his friends showed me a few moves that I could use for my strip dance. Chicago's had a neighboring female strip bar called Mugs and Jugs, and right when it was my turn to hit the stage and start stripping, I saw my brother and his friend sitting in Mugs and Jugs and looking over at Chicago's to see my performance. The amusing part was when my brother told me afterward that as he and his friend were looking over, everyone at Mugs and Jugs started questioning why they were watching the performance of the male strippers. This all happened back in the old times when people were not as liberal or open-minded as they are today. They did not know that my brother was simply there to see his brother's dance moves, but no one believed him even when he told them. I remember laughing in tears when he explained what happened to him and his friend that night.

Shortly after my brother returned from Toronto, we decided to move in together and rented a condo in Westminster. Our apartment building was quite centralized and surrounded by an area full of bars, restaurants, gyms, etc., at every street corner, making it the perfect place to live for us since it encompassed all our needs.

My brother and I had spent most of our lives in the same house until he moved out, but living in the same house with him, that, too, with just the two of us, was an interesting experience, to say the least. Being on our own, him in Toronto and me in college, we had learned to do a lot of chores around the house, so maintaining the condo wasn't a big issue.

However, I do remember getting into fights with him, mainly because I was very involved in bodybuilding by this time and had started to build a lot more muscle than him. Compared to me, his body was only getting heavier since he was gaining weight, and my body was becoming increasingly muscular and ripped. Therefore, I also gained much more attention from the ladies and began to sense a hint of jealousy in my brother. I understood his feelings because he was the sole reason why I started bodybuilding in the first place. I saw his ripped body and how popular he was among the ladies. He also challenged me, saying that I could never be better than him, which was the reason I started this activity in the first place. Now was the time when he could finally see me being more muscular and ripped than he ever was.

I joined my first bodybuilding competition, the Gators Classic, a local show in Vancouver, when I was 19. Despite being a local show, it was on a huge level. In the 80s and 90s, the Gators gym had made a huge name for itself throughout British Colombia. Therefore, well-known bodybuilders like Lou Ferrigno and various WWE wrestlers from all over British Colombia and nearby states flew into Vancouver to train there. So when I found out about the competition, I was hyped to join it. And when I finally decided to participate, I weighed around 240 lbs. After 12 weeks, when I stepped onto the stage, I weighed 175 lbs. How I managed to lose so much weight in such little time was a surprise for all but the person who helped me lose around 65 lbs. in 12 weeks - the owner of the Gator's Gym himself, Sergio. Sergio had trained and helped me prepare for the competition.

The result of the competition was that I was ranked third among a huge number of participants, and I was starstruck when I heard the news of my success. The main reason for that was that I was only 19 then, while my rivals' ages mostly ranged between the mid to late 20s. Therefore, I was delighted with my accomplishment with so much competition. It motivated me to compete again and be an even better bodybuilder.

While I was training, my brother became quite supportive of my interest in bodybuilding, but after I won the competition, he ended up becoming my biggest fan and was also extremely proud of me.

Apart from that, things were smooth sailing. My brother and I had always gotten along naturally since our childhood, and living with him was fun at most times. We hosted crazy parties in our condo and invited all our friends. We had our place now; we both loved to party and no longer feared our parents raiding us. So that's how most nights were at our place in Westminster. We occasionally spent the nights at the two bars down our street, which were Mugs and Jugs and Chicago's, the bar where I used to strip.

So, while my life wasn't ideal at this time, it also wasn't that bad either.

Chapter 5: First Job

Older siblings are considered to be the helpers of their younger siblings and their supporters. They look out for them and protect them. Usually, the former is more responsible and takes care of the latter. My older brother, on the contrary, always proved to be the complete opposite of that ever since my childhood. He was the reason I got in trouble; he would always be up to no good, and he managed to get me involved with him as well.

However, he was never the kind to rat me out, and he always supported me. The downside to that was that he supported me in bad things most of the time and eventually ended up getting involved with me. But I would still never consider him to be a bad older brother. He was the reason I had a fun childhood; he aroused my interest in bodybuilding and was my biggest supporter in all of my football games.

As we grew up, though, my brother Keith became more mature with time. He not only managed to get a decent, well-paying job right after his high school graduation but also moved out on his own. He eventually started behaving like an adult, and that is when his older sibling tendencies truly surfaced.

Keith worked for a bill collection agency called D. Appleton & Company in Toronto. He had worked hard and established himself as an important asset to the company. Afterward, he was transferred back to British Colombia, where the company had a better position for him. So, we ended up getting an apartment together in Vancouver since he was back. Using his higher position in the company and my state of unemployment, he got me a job in the same company.

At the time, I was struggling with odd jobs because college was expensive, and I was barely getting by. A proper job with a consistent paycheck was what I needed because until then, I was doing all kinds of odd jobs, as a tower guard or as a maintenance worker. I was 14 when I started working at Splashdown Park during my summer vacations.

Being a tower guard was fun since all I had to do was sit in one spot and give people a heads-up as to when it was all right for them to go down the slide. Another reason why I enjoyed this position was that, as a teenage boy, flirting with girls my age was exciting. Then, there were other parts of my job, like working as a maintenance worker, which were not as fun. The least enjoyable role was of the ground maintenance worker as you had to deal with garbage, bathrooms, and customers' complaints. Overall, these were all great first job experiences that taught me many lessons, like taking responsibility; of course, it got me a little bit of cash as well, but they were still odd jobs. I didn't plan on making a career out of them.

So, when I got the position of a skip tracer at the collection agency with the help of my brother, I was on cloud nine. It was my first experience in the corporate sector, my first full-time job ever. So, I was naturally nervous. However, I soon overcame the anxiety because everyone was really nice to me.

Getting a job at the collection agency was a bit difficult, considering I had only worked odd jobs so far. But I was able to get the job since my older brother had vouched for me. My job required me to do investigative research to track down a person who had not paid their bills to their creditors. Working there was a great experience for me. It was fun, and I soon became a pro at skip tracing, which helped me settle down nicely in the work environment.

Being a big, muscular guy, I had to keep bodybuilding and spent most of my time at the gym after work hours. Due to that, I also became the favorite of most of the women in the collection agency office. One time, my colleagues organized a Halloween party on the weekend. I got lucky and ended up kissing two of the women who worked there. At first, it was awkward because I saw them every day, but since no one talked about it afterward, I realized it was no big deal since we all were drunk that night.

Another reason I loved that job was that my brother and I worked together. Working with him was fun, and we could also attend work parties together as buddies and have lots of fun there. But, apart from that, the biggest benefit I had from working in the same company as my brother was that he drove us to and from work every day.

If I think about it, living with my brother was a rollercoaster. There were good times, and then there were crazy times. It was incredibly fun but also quite challenging at times. The fun part was when we hosted our parties since we were the only ones living in that condo. Since it was a small apartment, we could only host pre- or post-going-out parties because we could only have so many people over. Other than that, the pre-going-out parties included going to Mugs and Jugs or Chicago's afterward because they were the only bars near our apartment building.

My relationship with my brother was so fun that once, I purposely got us in a fight for the sake of fighting together. The fight occurred when we were in Chicago's one night. I had managed to impress a girl, who was now my date. My brother was also with us. As we were leaving, a guy came around and started flirting with my girl. Upon seeing that, my brother called him an idiot.

"What did you just say?" His response was quick.

That is when I jumped into the conversation and told him that my brother was calling him an idiot, and he instantly turned his head toward my brother. I did not mean to piss my brother off but rather the other guy because he was flirting with my date. But my brother decided not to mess with him and said, "Sorry, I didn't say anything."

After that, it seemed like everything was normal until the obnoxious idiot started flirting with my date again. My brother called him an idiot yet again, and the whole conversation repeated, giving me a déjà vu. Except this time, Keith did not defend himself when the guy went over to lay his hands on him. As he was about to hit him, I had the perfect chance to get my revenge. I jumped right in front of him, tossed him down, and all hell broke loose. All the guy's friends came over, and then my brother and I had to fight them all at once.

Despite being just two of us and being jumped by multiple guys, we escaped unscathed and also managed to hurt the other guy's friends pretty badly since one lay unconscious as we left. I remember we laughed about it a lot the next day.

After leaving the bar, my brother confronted me about why I did all that I did as we were walking home. My only response was, "You were the one who always wanted us to get into a fight together. So, when the perfect opportunity arose, why not use it?" Hearing this, my brother chuckled and hugged me. It was a warm, fun-filled moment for us brothers.

I remember that when we lived together, Keith used to interfere in my love life because we lived together, we worked together, and we almost always went out together. I spent most of my time with him, and he had the chance to influence me with his illogical advice somehow. And being the younger brother that I was, I always even ended up listening to him as well. This one time, I was dating an older woman; I did the same and listened to my brother.

The woman I was dating was 25, while I was 19. One particular night, he brought home a bunch of people to party with us, and one of them was an attractive girl who also happened to be interested in me. Since she was all over me and trying her best to seduce me, I held back, telling her that I had a girlfriend because I wanted to stay faithful to my lover. That is the part when my older brother jumped into the conversation and teased me by saying I was gay. He was trying to provoke me into having sex with the beautiful girl at the party, and after a lot of restraint, I gave in. It was not my finest hour, but I ended up spending the night with someone other than my girlfriend and felt horrible afterward. On the other hand, my older brother felt quite proud because he had finally managed to provoke me.

My brother and I spent so much time together at the bars that we eventually came up with the idea to start selling cocaine at these bars. The reason for that was that most people in Chicago's and Mugs and Jugs partook in that drug. However, our business could not survive for long since my brother soon became our top customer. I had to start hiding the cocaine from him, but he was already too addicted. One night, I had gone to sleep after storing the cocaine in a safe place because my brother had become a complete party animal. I was suddenly woken up by my brother rolling on the floor incredibly weirdly. For a second, I was on the verge of jumping out of bed in fear until I realized it was my brother. That's when I shouted at him, asking what he was doing. His hesitant reply was that he was simply looking for some cocaine because we had some "clients" who wanted it. I saw right through him, let out a laugh, and told him that I knew he would just sniff it with his friends. My brother, unable to accept that his younger brother had caught him, gave me a dumbfounded look and went away. So, the main reason that our business could not last long was because of my brother's addiction to it.

So, even after landing my first ever "real" job, thanks to my brother, my life continued to be wild.

Chapter 6: Losing My Path

Living the bachelor life together, my brother and I had the time of our lives. But, like always, life spins you in circles, and mine was sure to give me a hell of a ride as well. However, back then, I never took anything negatively, maybe because I was too young to understand the phrase, "Easy come, easy go."

I was about 21 years old when I got a "once in a lifetime" opportunity to make a lot of money for my age. It was by illegal means, however. Basically, I had found a way to make money by growing marijuana. Back then, it was illegal nationwide, but the temptation to make some dollars hit hard, and I grabbed the opportunity with both hands. It was like a carrot being dangled right in front of my face, telling me the potential of making a lot of money. For young adults like me back in the day, the competition was getting fierce, and everyone was busy paving the way to get some extra cash in their pockets.

It all started when I found out that one of my friends' brothers, Brandon, had started the same business. I came to know through Brandon himself that he already had a few locations where he was growing marijuana for his business. Then he went on to tell me how he had a whole network of people working for him; they would grow marijuana in their homes, supply it to him, and get paid monthly. That is when I got the hint that Brandon was offering me the chance to join his team and get into the small-scale business. So, we instantly made a deal: I would do hydroponics - a relatively easy way of gardening without soil, in the basement and get paid roughly $3k a month.

On top of that, I would be given a free place to live where I would carry out the operation.

Not having to pay rent and still having an extra three grand to take care of my troubles sounded too good to be true, but I wasn't much of a pessimist. I saw Brandon living a good, and I wanted that for myself as well. I was 21 years old at the time, and my mind was naive enough to overlook the consequences my actions could have in the future. As a youngblood full of curiosity and excitement, I couldn't care enough about all that could go wrong; my mind only rolled dollar signs in front of my eyes like a slot machine in a casino. Sometimes, when you see the money rolling in, you become blind to everything but the opportunity to make more dough than you are used to, which is what happened with me.

At that time, $3k was a huge amount of money for me, and I could not believe I was getting that kind of opportunity. Another reason for wanting in on the marijuana business was that I had seen Brandon and his friends in their fancy cars, always surrounded by lots of attractive women, and I wanted to be like them.

Ultimately, I took up the offer and started looking for house rentals, where conditions for cultivating marijuana would be perfect. Eventually, I found a place, and then the next step was to officially join Brandon's team. Sometime later, he also taught me how to take care of the plants; that is when I learned all I needed about the cultivation of marijuana within a closed boundary.

While I was working for Brandon, I still had my job at the Collection. Besides that, I continued my passion for bodybuilding and went to the gym regularly. Since I had no regular job and my working hours were flexible, I spent a lot more time at the gym.

While I was hitting the gym and doing proper bodybuilding, I was also working as a male stripper. I continued stripping because, after a while of working in the marijuana business, I discovered that money was never guaranteed and completely depended upon how much marijuana was produced. As far as I remember, I was paid $8k for eight weeks of work in the beginning. I was extremely happy and could not even decide where I should spend this money. However, soon afterward, things went downhill, and there came a time when I did not get paid for some months. At that time, I used to get extremely frustrated, but I still continued for some reason.

Due to the high degree of uncertainty in the marijuana business in terms of financial security, I decided to work as a male stripper at several nightclubs. So, life had become like this, where my entire routine included taking care of the marijuana plants, bodybuilding during the day, and stripping during the night. This continued for around 18 months, where I did hydroponics and stripped simultaneously.

At this point, I had realized college was not for me. I might have entered college with great enthusiasm when it first started, but once I got used to it, I lost my interest as well as the will to finish my degree. I was exposed to reality when I discovered the amount of studying and reading one had to do to pass the exams. Not only did I become overwhelmed by it, but I created a defense mechanism of simply giving up. I had become so negligent in my studies that my mother had to write my research papers for me. Due to my lack of interest in studies, I dropped out of college; however, at that stage of life, I realized it all happened for a reason and that teaching was not a suitable profession for someone like me.

So, there I was, a college dropout who was making OK money, albeit through various illegal and indecent means. At that time, the party life was at the forefront. So, the nights I used to strip were followed by partying at the bar with a few ladies who had previously attended the show.

The party life also led to a lot of alcohol and drug usage. That is when I completely drifted away from God, and my life went downhill. Drinking, getting high on drugs, and hanging around people who were involved in shady things were not a path to oneness with God. I got involved in things that were not good for my reputation, career, health, or my overall life and well-being. They could prove to be a pathway for my destruction in the end, but I kept going on the same track without considering the repercussions. I stopped praying and even talking to God. Money was the only religion for me. I wanted to be able to do whatever my heart desired, and there was only one way to make that happen: make a lot of dough. All that mattered to me at that point in life were women, money, the nightlife, and the gym. Everyone and everything else could take a hike for all I cared.

Even though I was making a lot of money, I was not financially stable. So, I had to move back in with my parents. I remember that when I moved in with them, my mother said something along the lines of, *"I would not mind as much if you had something to show for it."* I don't blame her, but it did sting a little.

My parents came to know about my stripping job in the most unexpected way. They found out that I had been working as a male stripper through my cousin, who told his father, and my uncle, who, in turn, told my parents about it. And how did I find out that they knew? It was when my dad put me on the spot while I was in a car with him one day.

While driving, he casually asked me, "So, how is the skin trade going?" At that moment, I realized that my father knew all about it, but I still tried to cover it up by saying things like, "It's not like that. We just wear shorts and serve drinks, Dad!" I was telling big lies to save myself from embarrassment, but I could tell that my dad wasn't buying it. I had never felt that embarrassed in my entire life, and I just wanted the ground to open up and swallow me whole to save me from that ordeal.

Looking back on my life, I realize how reckless my attitude was as I'd bring people to my house, where I used to grow marijuana plants. Anyone could have sold me out or been a rip-off, but back then, I could not care less. Also, because the main attraction of growing and stripping was living a lavish life with beautiful women and lots of money, I had completely forgotten about my safety and the future, let alone God and the concept of heaven and hell. On the other hand, there was one part of me that simply needed validation because I had always been an insecure person who was never confident in his skin. I had always craved admiration and validation, which I later received from stripping as women found me attractive. This was a partial reason why I remained associated with that work.

However, this side venture was just another small part of my life. Roughly six months into growing Marijuana, I decided to shut the doors of my stripping career. It was getting too much for me to handle physically. Those long nights of serving drinks and dancing for strangers hanging around the club, working a regular desk job, and growing Marijuana messed up the dial of my clock every day. Everyone else around me had a normal, less busy routine from which they could easily seek out the time for their leisure. In contrast, the hands of my clock spun faster than anyone else's. What someone might have called a "long day" was just a regular day for me. After the late nights started to wear me out and made me feel rundown, I ended my stripping career.

I did everything I could in order to get all the validation I needed. And somewhere along the way in fueling my desires, which mostly consisted of money, women, gym, and partying, I lost my way. At first, I was desperate to find a way to make more money. Hence, I was willing to do anything needed to fill my pockets. But as time marched on, I wanted to quit the drug business as I stopped fancying the time I spent with my employer. Also, I got frustrated as the prospects promised to me of growing Marijuana didn't work out as smoothly as I had expected. Evidently, I was receiving much less than I had hoped for. So, the Marijuana business slowly started to lose its sparkle.

Regardless of what happened later on in my Marijuana venture, I still do not regret it, or even stripping, for that matter. It's true that growing Marijuana and stripping made me grow up a lot faster than I should have, but they also gave me the opportunity to interact with different kinds of people. These folks weren't your average 9 to 5 people, but I definitely learned how to deal with all kinds of people, so that's something positive that came out of that.

Chapter 7: The First Downfall

"What goes up must come down." We have all heard that saying growing up, but the thing is that we don't really understand it until we experience our fall from grace. I wouldn't say that I was at the prime of my Marijuana growing business because business was slow, but I guess God decided I needed to be put back in place because I was eventually apprehended for my illegal business endeavors.

It was around 1998 when I got busted for growing Marijuana. It was the time when the product was moving in hot on the streets, and law enforcement considered it their Christmas, knowing all the arrests they could make. I eventually became a victim of their festive nature.

One day, I was at my parents' house when I heard a loud banging on the door. You can actually tell whether someone unusual or uninvited is standing on the other side just by the sound of knocking. Hence, when the house echoed with the loud knocks on the front door, my dad quickly went to answer it. I realized it was something serious when there was a sudden shift of soundwaves, from incessant banging to dead silence, and I could only hear my dad talking to some unidentified strangers across the house. After a brief conversation, my dad rushed into my room, angry and puzzled, and said, *"Son, what is this about a Marijuana grow op?"*

At that moment, I knew the jig was up, but I couldn't bring myself to admit it. I was dumbfounded as I was caught off guard that day. In my flustered state, my only response to my dad's inquiry was, "Um... I don't know." My dad proceeded to inform me that the police had come looking for me. There was a warrant out for my arrest, and this time, I had to give myself up. Since they had the paperwork, there was nothing he or any of us could do. The thought of calling a lawyer didn't even cross our minds at that moment.

Realizing I finally needed to come clean, I proceeded to drive toward the police station and turned myself in. It was a horrible feeling driving to the police station, not knowing what was going to happen to me. I also felt miserable because I had let my folks down. Now, I needed to carry that shame and do what was needed to set it right. This was my own fault because of my greed and lust. What could I do to salvage my reputation and regain my parents' trust?

Once I reached the police station, they started interrogating me. I knew I had no way to defend myself as the evidence of my crime could be found back at the apartment. But it went a lot easier than expected. I was expecting to be interrogated for my crimes, but all I had to do was provide my fingerprints. I was released on bail upon a promise to appear before the court.

The police officer who booked me was gentle, and he seemed genuinely concerned. He tried to make me understand that I was playing with the law and messing around with illegal stuff. He highlighted the fact that I did not have connections to organized crime and that I was raised in a respectable household. He tried to make me understand this. I think that I needed to leave it behind in order for me to realize that this life of crime was not for me.

I talked with my dad about what happened at the station. I think he sensed a change in me. He went on to assure me that despite being honest and respectful, he did not reveal anything to the police officers who came to arrest me. He just guaranteed them that he would talk to me and personally tell me to turn myself in.

I did not expect this because I thought my father would have been shocked at first and might have even given the cops free rein to do what they wanted. By asking the cops to politely leave and guaranteeing them that I would turn myself in, my father had de-escalated the situation and helped me be treated fairly.

Back at home, I felt horrible and embarrassed as I had nothing to say that would make things better. My father had a reputation in the community, and I had tainted it, which hurt me the most. While my dad dealt well with my blunder and had made peace with it, the worst thing for him was yet to come because, being the superintendent of the district, he had to let the school district board know about his son's transgressions with the law. How he faced the board and his social circle, I don't know. I can't even begin to imagine the torture and horror he went through.

Now that my operation had been busted and I had nowhere to go, I was forced to move back in with my parents. However, I wasn't as welcome as I would be under different circumstances. I again remembered my mother saying, *"I would not mind what you did if you actually had something to show for it."* That was a moment filled with stress and anxiety as I couldn't see past it. My thoughts were distressed and unclear; I couldn't think straight about my next course of action. I let my parents down, and the whole incident with the police was the ultimate sledgehammer that tore down their respect. That was not even the worst part; I didn't even have much cash on me at that time, which eventually added to the stress.

In times of such stress, I would think about how my whole operation was busted and what I could have done differently, but looking back, it was only a matter of time before someone found out.

When I returned home from the station that day, I learned that my marijuana operation had been suspected by a neighbor who proceeded to report suspicious activity to the police. The police then put my home under surveillance after the tip and eventually found out I used to steal power from the grid for my operations. After confirmation of their suspicions, the police issued their warrant to raid my home and arrest me for gathering further information and evidence.

At first, the thought of getting a lawyer didn't even cross anyone's mind. However, as I came to terms with the situation, I realized that I was about to be branded with some serious jail time, and now that I was thinking a bit more clearly, my next move was to get a lawyer for myself. My dad was the only one who could afford a lawyer then, and he was kind enough to hire one to get me out of the rut I was in.

Luckily, a friend of mine referred a top lawyer to me from Vancouver. I made a phone call to him to set up an appointment. My dad also did some research on his own and agreed that the lawyer from Vancouver was true to his reputation. His name was Mr. Tarnow, and he was an expensive litigator to deal with.

When I first met Mr. Tarnow, I was told the prosecutors were seeking to demand two years of imprisonment for me. I was horrified. I nearly shit my pants when I heard that. Before we even went to court, our legal aid had cost us over $17,000! I knew the expenses during the trial would skyrocket, and I would have to arrange a lot of money which I did not have.

Given my situation, my lawyer advised me to plead guilty because it would help save me from the huge costs that would arise during trial, and my sentence might even get reduced. There was nothing to lose, and I wanted it to end soon; I wanted relief for my family.

I had no prior convictions or accusations, so the court went easy on me, and for the duration of the legal proceedings, I was allowed to live my life, the only restriction being that I was not allowed to leave the country.

I decided I would plead guilty, and my lawyer would try to see if I could receive no jail time and save my dad from any other legal costs. Mr. Tarnow reached out to the prosecutor and tried to negotiate a deal with him. He was successful. I was offered six months' probation if I pleaded guilty. Once I spent this time as an honest, law-abiding citizen, my sentence would be over, and I would be a free man. I gladly agreed.

It was weird listening to the judge sentence me in court while my dad was sitting right behind me on the benches. My dad played a big role in me seemingly getting away with a slap on the wrist. Because my dad was a well-respected and recognized member of the community, he played a key role in my getting only six months of probation from the court. The judge realized that things like these could potentially break a family apart, so he gave my dad a pat on the back for being there for his son in his darkest hour.

According to my probation terms, I had to devote a certain number of hours to community service. I also had to pay back $3000 to the landlords of the house that I rented for growing Marijuana. I also had to visit my probation officer at least once a month, where I would witness all sorts of people. I felt out of place, luckily, and happy that my life was about to be sorted. I did not want to associate with such people or be involved in a life of crime. A lot of criminals or alleged offenders seemed to have ongoing drug addiction issues. I thanked God and continued visiting the probation officer.

My probation period was fairly easy because I got a job at a company called Searchmaster. I was employed as a skip tracer, searching for people who skipped out on debts to creditors.

It did take me a while to get used to living with my parents again, though. However, with time, I began to enjoy my life, reminiscent of the old days, having to follow my folks' rules. They used to go to bed early, and as long as I was under their roof, I did not have permission to stay out late at night. I had found a new normal, living the life of a hard-working and clean citizen. It was all about simply working, eating, sleeping, and repeating.

This was the first and most significant downfall in my life for me. I hoped that by the end of my probation, I would be a changed man. Unfortunately, the universe had other plans for me.

Chapter 8: Trouble Staying Sober

As the judge banged the gavel, all hell broke loose. This was the point where life went downhill, and there was nothing I could do to make it right other than suffer the consequences. I got knocked into a different life in ways I couldn't even imagine.

After pleading guilty, I was not allowed by the United States government on their soil for the next ten years before I could file for a waiver or a Canadian pardon. During that time period, I was working as a skip tracer. I moved out from my parent's house and rented a basement suite with another friend, who was also a skip tracer like me. I also considered it better to move out of my family's home as there was already a negative aura surrounding the house complemented by me – I wouldn't say I liked the feeling of looking guilty as I saw their faces.

The company we worked for, The Searchmaster, facilitated their employees by allowing them to work from home. Our work was assessed on a performance-enhanced basis. I also started hitting the gym, lifting weights, and pumping myself up. It was always good to have regular training to be part of your routine. As it happens, it didn't take me long to switch to high-intensity exercise and bodybuilding – I was slowly becoming a gym freak then.

I was also seeing someone from the United States so I was managing a long-distance romance. Shortly after I got convicted, I had doubts clouding my mind, whispering that things might be over between us or at least get bumpy. I put her on a call and asked her whether she could move to Canada with me or if she would be seeing me again. I remember when I visited her one time, we went and saw a medium where it was mentioned to me that a black-haired woman would soon be instrumental in my life. We looked at each other and just shrugged it off. However, she wasn't the one I would tie the knot with.

It was on my 26th birthday when destiny called for me. My ex-girlfriend, Darlene, invited me out one evening to celebrate my birthday. She planned it all by herself, trying to make it memorable for me. Darlene had friends who wanted to go to the bar to celebrate. She wanted me to meet one of her friends whom she thought I might admire. Without even playing hard to get in front of her, I accepted the invitation right off the bat. We entered the bar, had a couple of drinks, laughed, and had a great time until she called out the lady she wanted to introduce to me. "Atira!" she called for her in a raised pitch.

Not moments after saying 'hi' to her, we picked a corner where we started talking to each other like crazy. We spoke as if there was no one else present inside the room, and the flow of our conversation seemed endless. We kept staring into each other's eyes for the rest of the evening, hoping that the night would never end. As it turns out, she woke up next to me the following morning. She left after having breakfast, but I remember I wanted to see her again so badly as soon as she left.

At this point, I realized that I had to end things with the lady in the United States. She was not so happy about my decision, but we both realized that certain things are not in our control. And the distance was one of the significant factors that weakened our bond; my situation at that time only made things worse for us.

Atira was an intelligent soul – I was impressed by her quick-witted nature and how she had her way with words. She worked for a marketing company for which she attended college. Although she was very petite, she had that 'larger than life' persona – many would refer to her as the 'firecracker.' Whilst we dated, we both had the same energy toward each other and continued dating after the first time we met. She lived in a small, one-bedroom apartment in New Westminster – It took me by surprise that she was living in the same building where my brother and I lived six years earlier. She was also good company when she was around; she made me laugh and ensured everyone was in a good mood.

After we dated for a while, we introduced our parents to each other. We even trained together; we used to go to Gator's gym after work, which was the best gym in town. Those times were hard in terms of earning money. Atira and I realized our financial standpoint, so we both said to each other, "If we only had $20,000, we would be set."

After three months of dating and pure excitement, I moved into her apartment. It was a small dwelling, but I wouldn't complain about it. Eventually, things got a little hard for us financially. I had a Ford Ranger pickup truck – its transmission was busted, and I needed about $1800 to fix it. Neither of us had the extra money coming to us, so I had to borrow it from my dad and pay him back after some time. At this point, we realized that we both wanted to find an additional revenue stream to pay for our cheques. The money we had coming in wasn't enough for any extraordinary expenses popping up. We ran the house purely on budget.

A friend of mine, Dick, approached me during that time and asked whether I wanted to live in his weed-growing op and get paid for doing it. He said that we would be paid five to ten grand extra every month. The offer was highly tempting at that time when our pockets were way lighter than before. At first, I remember being hesitant when the request was presented in front of me since I already had a criminal record for being involved in the same thing. I consulted Atira about this, and she was all about it – it went much better than I thought it would. After seeing the money, I decided we would go check out the place before making the final decision – and then we jumped on the bandwagon. It was apparent that I shouldn't tell my parents about it, considering what I'd put them through. Not having enough money to fix the truck was the only thing that led me to go back to the weed-growing operation.

I still remember how nervous I was about the idea but broke enough to change my mind. It pushed me to do it again. It was like Christmas all over again, without realizing that I was dancing on quicksand.

Chapter 9: The Big Operation

Marriage is a sacred bond that unites two people together. It may seem like a very daunting task at first and a very monumental decision, which it surely is, but one that can bring you much peace and happiness if you choose the right person to spend your life with.

Being in a relationship with Atira was a thrilling moment for me. It was the right kind of change I needed in my life. And so, after being together for just about a year, I decided to pop the big question.

We can all agree that proposals are extremely passionate and emotional occasions. It is a big deal to choose the person you are going to spend the rest of your life with and possibly the most important decision you can ever make in your life. I felt like I was ready to take our relationship to the next level. It was a weird feeling, as I was experiencing different emotions all at once: excitement, nervousness, happiness, and anxiousness. Nevertheless, I overcame the emotions and spent a lot of time thinking about how I would go about it.

Once I had thought about it enough, I bought a flower and went straight to Atira's workplace. As soon as I entered, I handed it over to her, got down on my knee, and asked her if she would marry me in front of the whole staff. Although she felt embarrassed that I had proposed in front of everyone, fortunately, she said yes.

I proposed to Atira in 2002, and we got married in 2003. Since both of us were broke and didn't have enough money for the wedding celebrations, we decided to have a small wedding. However, my dad was kind enough to jump in and pay for the other necessary wedding expenses.

Since my dad was the one funding the wedding, we searched for the perfect place to be our wedding venue within the budget. In the end, we settled for VanDusen Garden. It is a beautiful garden in Vancouver, consisting of 55 acres of greenery, lakes, and waterfalls – the ideal destination for a small yet magical wedding.

We exchanged our wedding vows amidst the beautiful garden setting. I remember roughly 30 people being at our wedding. It was all so beautiful, with the well-trimmed lawns, floral atmosphere, vast grounds, and flowerbeds and rosebushes. The natural and floral embellishments on the venue were the epitome of elegance and beauty. It was truly a worlds-away feeling for us because of the abundance of floral arrangements and lush green surroundings. My brother, who was my best man, and Atira's sister, who was the maid of honor, were standing beside both of us with happy faces, supporting our decision to publicly accept and declare our love for one another.

As much fun and great as that day was, it was also a long and tiring one, even though it was a small affair. At the end of the day, we said our goodbyes to everyone and went straight to the hotel where we were going to stay. Shortly after entering the hotel, the chauffeur led us to our room, and we were so tired that as soon as we got inside our room, both of us just fell on the bed and slept for ages.

At the time, I asked Atira to marry me, and I was living in a 500-square-foot apartment. However, soon after proposing, I realized we needed a bigger place as we were starting a new chapter of our lives and possibly a new family. Then, both of us combined made just enough to get by, so the urge to make more money became more intense.

Marriage often brings with it changes in your personality and how you perceive the world. For me personally, being a married man didn't change me much besides feeling like I had to provide for and support my wife. This made me a more responsible man, and I tried to look for ways to make more money and gain a better lifestyle for both of us. No matter which religion or culture you belong to, every husband makes a vow to fulfill his wife's needs, both emotional and financial, so it was a great deal for me to take care of Atira's needs and earn for her.

So, as time went by, the escalated sense of fulfilling the needs of my wife encouraged me to make more money. I tried to do everything I could to make good money. I had become a completely different man after marriage. I became responsible and punctual with hopes and dreams of becoming successful and rich one day.

In my quest to make more money, I unknowingly (or perhaps deep down, I was aware of it) fell down the rabbit hole again. Amidst all the hardships we were facing, I finally got an opportunity to make money fast. My friend, Dick, offered me to join a grow-op, and the offer was particularly striking because we would get paid just to live there.

Dick used to work for a man who went by the name of Slick and asked me to join him, too. Most of these guys used nicknames, and only the ones who had worked with them or for them for a while were privy to their actual names. Anyway, after getting the offer, Atira and I went to check out our new accommodation.

It was a somewhat small grow-op operating from the basement of a 5000 sq ft house, and since we were just required to live upstairs and could go about our lives as usual, we immediately accepted the offer. Not only would we get paid, but we could also save the money we were spending on paying rent.

In the middle of this ongoing operation, our role was to just live there. We lived upstairs while the drugs were grown in the basement. We maintained our routine there; we used to get up in the morning, go to our respective jobs, and then come back and stay at the place at night. In conclusion, we had nothing to do with the actual operation and just carried on with our normal routines.

It was Dick who was in charge of the operation; he had to handle all the issues that arose and make sure that everything went on smoothly. However, how can you handle an issue if you aren't there when it occurs? My friend had a bit of a drug problem, so it was common for him to not be around a lot of the time.

One evening, out of the blue, Slick called me up to tell me he was coming by to see how things were going. As soon as he entered, he went straight to the basement.

"How often does Dick come around?" he asked me as I followed him downstairs.

I didn't expect this question, so I got confused and stayed silent for a moment, wondering how I should answer.

"Ummm…" I began, but to be honest, I didn't know what to say. Dick was my friend, but Slick was the boss. I was in a difficult situation.

Slick figured out that I was about to lie and save my friend from the humiliation he was going to face if I spoke the truth.

"Don't lie to me," Slick said as if he was certain that Dick wasn't working properly, and he was often not present to overlook the operation.

Realizing Slick could probably see through my lies, I decided to tell him the truth. "Not very often," I blurted, looking down.

As soon as he heard that Dick wasn't taking this seriously, right there and then, he said something that took me by surprise. He said, "Okay, you're the one that is gonna run the place from now on."

I didn't know how to react to that. It was a huge opportunity for me, and I became nervous and excited at the same time, thinking about what this could lead to. I had to do some serious thinking. I couldn't just let go of this opportunity; I could see my future with Atira in a big house with enough money to cover our expenses as well as luxuries.

After a discussion with my wife, which did not require a lot of convincing, I agreed to handle the operation. I was looking forward to taking this operation on the road to success.

The grow op went on for about a year before we had to shut it down due to power issues. After it closed down, I remember running into Dick and Slick at the gym one day. Slick offered me a new job at a much bigger operation than the previous one. For this new gig, I had to work only on the weekends, but the catch was that I was not allowed to leave the place while on duty as the place ran on a diesel generator. So, I had to make sure that I was there at all times to make sure it was running properly. This way, they would be off the power grid and not easy for the authorities to find.

Although we were making good money thanks to the grow-op, it came with a price. Out of the 5000 sq ft, we only got about 200 sq ft for living, while the rest of the area in the house was used for the operation - for growing the weeds and the generator. I can still remember the humming of the generator that wouldn't let us sleep peacefully at night. It was a massive generator, roughly 300 kilowatts, and stood about 7 feet high and 8 feet long to power up the whole 5000 sq ft grow-op. To an unsuspecting passerby, the place appeared to be just a really large house, but inside, it was a factory pumping out weed.

Of course, managing the growing op was no easy task. It was a lot of work, and I remember one of the guys who worked there asking me in the initial days if I was cut out for the job. After that exchange, I remember looking in the mirror and saying to myself, "You got this. You can do this." I convinced myself that even though it was a lot of work, I had the potential to handle it.

A lot was riding on this gig: Atira's future and mine, as well as our comfortable lives. And so, I did the best I could and gave it my all. Soon enough, the efforts I put in proved to be fruitful, and within a year, I was promoted to the main supervisor position. I ran the place with an iron fist and was answerable to Slick only. I remember that while I was the supervisor, roughly six other employees worked there, looking after various parts of the operation, from the plants to the air conditioning to the generator.

Dick wasn't too pleased when I got the job opportunity before him, as he was the one who introduced me to Slick and gave me a shot at the grow-op. However, Slick was all about having responsible people run his operation, and he knew that I would work to my full potential. So, he gave me another shot as he thought I would be a better resource than Dick. Slick trusted me more than Dick, and because of that, Dick and my relationship became strained for a couple of years after that.

Who doesn't want to change their life and find their way out of poverty one way or another? So, I couldn't have possibly denied this huge opportunity. But there was one question in my mind: What was coming for me in this big operation: money, success, or misfortune? I didn't know the answer to these questions then; all I knew was that Slick wanted me to start right away, and this was another great opportunity for me, so I agreed to this life-changing opportunity. I told Atira about how we had a great chance of making good money, and as I had guessed, she was okay with me doing it because she also knew we were in dire need of some extra cash.

After getting this opportunity, my lifestyle changed drastically. I was in charge of a big operation and was making loads of money. Because of the grow-op, I was able to buy my first house, get nice cars for myself and Atira, and go on great vacations.

My parents' role in my life cannot be understated. They were my pillars of guidance, support, and love. So, one of the very first things I did after the business took off was take them on a trip to Mexico. Although there is no way I can ever pay them back for everything they have done for me, it was my way of paying back my dad for covering my lawyer bills a few years earlier when I got busted.

Returning to the marijuana growing game was my own decision, but sometimes, it still surprised me that after going through all that, my sentence in jail, and being declared guilty in front of everyone - especially my parents, I relapsed and went back to my old habits without thinking about the consequences. I wasn't proud of what I did, but what other option did I have to make good money?

"Poverty is the parent of revolution and crime."

-Aristotle

Chapter 10: The Ultimate Loss

December 24, 2009, Christmas Eve was one of the best nights. Like any other family, it was our favorite time to spend together. We decorated our house with lights and other accessories along with a beautiful Christmas tree, which was also decorated with lights and ornaments.

We went out for a family dinner at Chops Steakhouse to celebrate Christmas. The whole city reflected happiness as the streets were lit up with beautiful Christmas decorations, sparking joy among people. By this time, I had ventured out on my own and was my own boss. I had learned from Slick the ins and outs of running a growing operation as well as the stress that comes along with it.

As we drove past the neighborhood, we saw all the houses decorated, and each individual we saw was full of happiness. We saw bells, reindeer, candles, and various other ornaments hanging on the doors of houses, shops, and restaurants. Colorful lights were lined on the rooftops and windows. The bristly wreaths were hanging on the front doors. We even spotted a glow-up Santa and his fleet of perfectly arched reindeer on a front lawn.

As we reached Chops Steakhouse, we ordered appetizers. The waiter had just brought our appetizer when I got a call from Vonn, my employee at the Grow OP property. As soon as I picked up the call, all I could hear was "FIRE!"

Hearing that, my anxiety levels shot up, and I asked him what he was talking about. "There's a fire in the generator room,"

Vonn replied. My heart started pounding, and I felt like I was sinking into my chair. My overwhelmed expression gave away the fact that something bad had happened; everyone at the dinner table could tell and was now alerted.

I felt a huge wave of shock, and it felt like I had no power or control over what was about to happen in my life; I could see my future burned into ashes.

As we drove back home, I could see the smoke from afar, and the whole town could see how huge the fire was. Industrial-sized generators were installed on that property so the operation could go on smoothly, but who knew that the whole production would be lost due to the same generators that were installed to make the operation effective and efficient?

The fire started from the basement and soon spread to the first floor until the flames engulfed the whole house. I could see the ravaging flames destroying my years of work in mere seconds. My house and business were both ablaze in front of me, and I stood there helpless while the massive fire scorched the whole property.

Fortunately, no one was hurt as the employees took off from the scene before the fire brigade arrived. The firefighters were trying to put out the massive blaze that engulfed the property as we reached there. Although the firefighters and other rescue teams were able to control the massive fire, I lost everything in the process.

I faced a great financial loss because of the fire. I paid a hefty sum for city fines, clean-up of the property, and mortgage coverage. I had to pay all of the fines from my pocket as there was no business anymore. Just the post-fire clean-up alone cost me a substantial sum.

Luckily, it was Christmas Eve, and the skeleton crew was there, so no real investigation took place on the property, nor did the police get involved.

Finally, something good was going on in my life, and I had started to make money, but now it had slipped from my hands in the form of ashes. What was supposed to be the happiest night of the year became a tragic one for me.

***

Soon after the fire incident in 2010, I purchased a new property in Aldergrove, a small community within the Township of Langley. Located at the southeastern edge of both the Greater Vancouver metropolitan area and the Township of Langley, Aldergrove is located near the western edge of the Abbotsford metropolitan area.

Many people think it's a town unto itself, but it has not been incorporated. The property was spread over 5 acres, and it was private, with no neighbors around. "Out of sight, out of mind" was always my motto and it was the perfect spot for a grow-op farm.

As there were no neighbors, there was no one to see the operation I was conducting on the property. I was glad that after suffering such a big loss, there was nobody here who would be a threat to my new operations. The property was heavily guarded with lush stands of alder trees. It was a peaceful community of farmers, and everyone kept to themselves. I was at ease, knowing that there were no nosey neighbors around my property who would interrupt my business.

For a year, my business in Aldergrove went well, but that was soon going to change. At the beginning of 2011, in January, I was driving back home when my phone rang. As I answered the call, the first thing I heard was, "Is that your property on the news right now?" It was a friend of mine.

It was then that I came to know that the new property I had purchased less than a year ago had been subjected to a police raid. It was all over the news; the police officers were giving interviews that this was a prime crime location and highly organized crime had been going on there for a while. Not only that, but they also mentioned that they could never have found out about the place if they had not received a tip.

I came to know that an employee I had hired for security on the property, Paddy, had ratted out the operation to the police. Unbeknownst to me or the others, Paddy was involved in a murder case before I hired him. The police had scooped him up off of the work site.

Paddy must have come under pressure and told them about the property of the grow-op, which led to surveillance on the property. It was a huge raid that resulted in four people being arrested.

This incident left me with nothing but pain; I had to face a huge financial loss yet again. I was so traumatized that often, I felt like putting my head in the sand and never taking it out. I remember I lost approximately $310,000 this time around, which included the loss from the halting of the operations and the lawyer's fee. Although I did not go to jail, one of the workers, Hoss, pleaded guilty and got one-year probation, while everyone else got off with a slap on the wrist.

I was glad that Atira was by my side during these troubling times. She was really supportive of me as I dealt with the tragedies that were coming to me one by one. Atira knew very well the ins and outs and the risks the business involved, yet she stood by my side and supported my decision each time.

Meanwhile, I took on another project and started a family business. We called it "doitfordollars." The idea was originally mine and my brother's as he was well-versed in technology and computer savvy. He had all the ideas while I financed the project to establish it. I was only left with a little bit of money to invest, but there was no other way that could lead us out of the financial troubles except for this, so I invested all of my money in it.

Atira also jumped on board in the family business to look after the money I invested, as she was the person my brother and I trusted the most with our finances. The idea of that business was like the water bucket challenge but with compensation. It was like you got dared, and if you conquered the challenge, you were compensated for it.

Unfortunately, my brother was a spendthrift; he recklessly wasted money. He was not the one who would save money but someone who bought nonessentials and viewed spending freely as his "right." However, the problem was that none of the money was his; the money invested in the business was all that I was left with. My brother wanted the best of everything, whether it be cars, an expensive website, or expensive marketing for the business. Due to the extravagant expenses, we had to reach out to other investors as well; we could see the business was doomed from that moment forward.

Unfortunately, the business never got established, which caused a lot of angst between me and my brother. The failure in the business resulted in my brother walking out on the business as he developed a drug addiction. Due to his condition, we had to send him to the rehabilitation center, causing a lot of strain on the family.

I lost a huge amount of money in the process of marketing and creating fancy websites, but the business never made money, and eventually, it ended up causing a huge loss to everyone involved. Many investors felt ripped off and even accused me of scamming them when, all in all, the business just went down because of extravagant spending on marketing and other aspects that did not derive financial return.

It was an extremely stressful time for me as the gnawing failure haunted my every living moment. I wanted to get rid of the terrible thoughts. So, as a coping mechanism, I developed the habit of drinking and started doing cocaine often.

Doing drugs and drinking alcohol had become my escape and an attempt to drown my sorrows. It gave me a fleeting feeling of intense excitement, making me forget about my troubles.

I got to the point where I would be drinking and snorting cocaine multiple times a week. I trapped myself in a fantasy that it was not that big of a deal as I was still functioning and taking care of business, or at least what was left of it. But little did I know that this routine was only increasing my miseries that were to last long.

The stress led me to the point where I deliberately tried to ruin myself by indulging in substance abuse. Somewhere in between the vicious use of drugs and alcohol, I lost my spirituality, and I felt that my negative habits pushed me away from God.

However, despite all that, I felt bad deep down inside, like something was holding me down, pulling me away from my family. Was all hope lost, or did I still have a chance to turn my life around?

Chapter 11: The Accident

The summer of 2014 was marked by a new beginning and an attempt to change our lives. Atira and I went on a vacation to our summer house in Osoyoos, which is a small town in British Columbia that is classified as the only desert in Canada. The town was absolutely gorgeous, from the rugged hills and mountains all the way to sandy lakeshores and rolling vineyards, all provided plenty of beautiful sights.

As we stepped outside the car, we felt the warmth and positive energy of the summer, and the calm and peaceful ambiance radiated tranquility. With the clear blue sky, the day was radiant, peaceful, and lovely as the golden sun shone above our heads.

Constructed with redwood and treated timber, the summerhouse stood in front of the lake, perfectly appealing to one's eyes with no deviations or defects. It was an enclosed place, light and airy, but somewhat shielded from the sun as it gets extremely hot in Osoyoos in the summer, with temperatures reaching almost 40°C.

At this point in time, I was still involved in substance abuse, and my addiction only escalated over time. I can tell you that alcohol dulled my brain and ultimately led to a loss of self-control.

I had a habit of drinking and going down, doing the splits for fun when I was boozed up. Well, that summer of 2014 was the last time I attempted that in my life.

One evening, we decided to go to the local pub in Osoyoos named "The Sage," a place where people would go for drinks, dance, and have a good party. Music was being played by a live band, and the drink menu was fun, so I got carried away with the flow and drank much more than I should have.

Being intoxicated, I was befuddled, and the only thing I could hear was the ladies at the club egging me to do the splits. I could also hear Atira saying, "Don't do it," standing behind me, but her voice faded with all the encouraging shouts I was hearing from other ladies. As I was too numb to understand my wife, I went down and did the splits.

When I jumped back up after my great performance, the crowd yelled, "One more time!" and down, I went to please the strangers and entertain them. As I bent down while doing the splits for a second time, I heard a loud popping sound.

Somehow, I got up and sat on a chair. However, I was in immense pain and remained on the chair for the rest of the night. The audience I was entertaining became disappointed, and I heard them whispering, "Okay! It's time to go." I tried to get up from the chair, but the attempt failed and added more pain to the misery I was feeling at the time.

When the time came to go home, I could not stand up, so two people had to take me home from the club. Unbeknownst to me at the time, I had completely severed my hamstring tendon - it was cut off 6 cm down the tendon.

The hamstring tendons are the strong bands of tissues at the back of the thighs, attaching the large thigh muscle to the bone from the hip all the way below to the knee.

After that accident, I could not walk for several months. The doctor even said that I would never be able to compete in bodybuilding again as my leg was severely damaged. My swollen and bruised leg made it impossible to walk or even stand up on my own.

It was a long road to recovery, and it took seven months to heal my leg. I remember the time when I tried to stand up and ended up in extreme pain. I felt a sudden sharp pain in the back of my thigh, and the next thing I knew, there was blood rolling down the inside of my leg. I could not bear the pain and fainted on the floor.

It was the most painful time of my life because, during this time, Atira and I were growing further apart from each other as she was focused on the business and the new opportunities coming to her while I was going further down the dark path. I was injured, I could not walk on my own, and I was stressed with all the misfortunes in my life, so I started abusing drugs and alcohol even more. What else was I supposed to do? I was an injured, hopeless man with no hope left because being wasted seemed the only way that could numb the pain I was going through, both physically and mentally.

Atira and I owned a property in the suburb of Langley, where we had been living since 2009, called Willoughby. I remained in the house while Atira tried to save the business we started with my brother. She transformed it into a social media marketing company and named it Viraltech.

She was invested in work and wanted to save it at any cost. She used to commute for 2 to 2.5 hours each day from Langley to downtown Vancouver to work. She only had two employees in the company, but she wanted to expand the business, so she started meeting investors. She climbed the ladder of business in an attempt to become the businesswoman she knew she had the potential to be.

The failure of the business that was caused due to my brother's carelessness lingered in our married life as well. Atira started to remain unhappy; she was fed up and wanted to move from Langley to downtown Vancouver.

Our marriage came under strain due to the financial losses we faced over the years. So, we made a decision to move, rented our place in Langley, and moved to Vancouver. Although I was farther from my work in Langley, her workplace was closer now. I was ready to make the sacrifice if it meant it would keep the family together.

The apartment we moved into was in a posh area called Coal Harbor. It was a 2-bedroom, 2-bathroom suite. Atira was happy that she was closer to work and that the apartment was everything she wanted. However, my endeavors remained futile in saving our relationship as we grew apart over time.

It is easy for couples to grow apart, particularly when each of them has responsibilities and commitments pulling them in opposite directions. Without realizing it, Atira was going on a different path, which led to a point where she felt disconnected from me. The worry of becoming strangers added stress to our relationship, and the worst part was when she constantly denied that we were growing apart.

I must mention that there were many moments of realization at that point where I thought about changing my life for the better, making amends for the past, and leaving behind my drinking habit. But when it comes to cutting back on alcohol, the darkness pulls you back into the dark hole.

Any time I tried to cut back on alcohol, my body would go through withdrawals, and I'd take a swig straight out of the pint. I was falling down the dark hole of destruction, and I knew if I kept on that path, I would kill myself.

I felt a dark force pulling me as weird things started to happen in my house. I remember the day that still gave me goosebumps when my son walked into my bedroom and said, "Dad, it's really heavy in here, and it's hard to breathe." Not only this, but I used to wake up in the middle of the night with deep scratches on my body, specifically on the back of my shoulders. It felt as if Freddy Krueger had clawed me.

Something terrible was happening in my house, and it became so extreme and deathly that I could not sleep at night. I remember one night when I could not sleep in my bed, so I went into the living room to sleep on the couch. As I sat on the couch, an ornament that was hung on the wall came flying at me as if someone had thrown it with extreme force, clearly with the intention of hurting me.

That did not stop there; it even hurt Atira. I remember one morning, she was lying down at the edge of the bed and had two large bruises around her ankles.

Anytime an individual gives in to substance abuse in an attempt to fill the emptiness in their soul, they open a portal to evil. This is the reason it is hard for people to break the addiction.

We must remember that we are spiritual beings in a human vessel, and we were created to serve God, not the devil. The dark side wants our souls, so we must not play with our minds and bodies by drinking alcohol.

I can recall another deadly incident when I was cooking dinner in the kitchen with Atira when suddenly I felt that my arm was burning. I tilted my head to see what was happening and saw three demonic scratches that had appeared on my arm.

That was the incident that made me decide I needed to change my habits. Memories of my drunken behavior started to horrify me; I knew my life was in shambles as I felt ashamed and broken.

However, I could not pull myself out of the darkness. I could not quit drinking on my own, and I needed help. Not just a rehabilitation center help, but something more than that, something spiritual.

Chapter 12: Repairing

One of the most common goals among individuals is to become a better version of oneself. Not just once but many times in life, we get hit by severe tragedies and difficulties that seem to challenge our peace. But they only exist to allow us to learn through them how we can grow and become better humans. There came a point in my life when fate landed me in such a situation where I was tested in every sense of the word.

Because of the paranormal things that were occurring in my apartment, I was losing my peace of mind. So, one day, I reached out to one of my best and life-long friends, 'BigD.' I asked him whether he believed in spiritual stuff, which he acknowledged. I explained what was happening in my apartment and how it was becoming extremely difficult for me to continue living there. He was appalled when I told him the story of how the ornament came flying at me or the scratches and other things I had encountered in the last few months. The first thing he did was give me the number of his spiritual mentor, 'Lori.'

I quickly reached out to her and explained what was happening. We eventually made an appointment for her to come over to my apartment for an investigation. On the agreed-upon day, someone rang the bell, and I answered the door only to find a hippie-looking woman with long red hair and a calm and decent demeanor standing there. After exchanging pleasantries, I invited her in.

As soon as she walked into my place, she started to look around and started coughing. She kept on coughing as she moved from one room to another. She looked at me and asked whether I did cocaine or any other drug. It was obviously embarrassing - I hummed and hawed and let out an occasional "yes" from time to time.

After a thorough examination, she started explaining to me whatever was in my apartment was very dark, and I realized that deep down, I wanted to make a change for the better. But that darkness did not want that, so the scratches were to stress me out. I knew that whenever I got stressed out, I would resort to drinking and abusing drugs to get away from it all.

After she explained to me what was happening, she brought in drums. She burnt sage in every corner of the place and performed a ceremony to hopefully get rid of the evil energy. She also suggested bringing love back into my life, as darkness would not be able to stand light and love.

As Lori guided me, it felt like I was shedding my skin as a snake would. It felt like a new me was being born – a phoenix rising from the ashes. As light and love came back into my life, there were so many signs showing that I was going through a spiritual awakening.

I also remember the day after Lori left, there were signs of it. We lived on the 20th floor, and I remember looking out the window and there was a white feather stuck in the building's window. I stayed there for about ten days as I was getting better and better, and the place was feeling lighter. There was a huge weight being laid off from my chest. One day, I noticed that the feather was gone and realized it was the best I had felt in a long time.

When I got in touch with Lori again, she explained to me that the feather was a sign that angels were looking after me and no dark energy would be able to bother me anymore. I did not require a rehabilitation center or therapy for my alcohol and cocaine addiction; it surprisingly went away. There was no urge anymore as my heart felt fulfilled. I wasn't feeling empty anymore; all I felt was immense love flowing through my body. It was a wonderful feeling.

As this process went on, I started reading spiritual books like there was no tomorrow. If someone had suggested one to me before this incident, I would have considered it nonsense. But now, everything made sense to me as I turned the pages. I was scanning through them weekly, taking in all the information I could. I felt so blessed that God had saved me from the darkness.

Needless to say, I was very grateful to Lori for making me wary of the darkness and coming into alignment with God again. Looking back, I realize that fighting through darkness is no joke. We hear about murders and suicides, often where people kill their families and themselves. We hear about people succumbing to a lifelong addiction that spreads like cancer throughout their bodies. Their body eventually rusts away and falls apart. After going through what I went through, it all made sense.

By the fall of 2015, I could say that I was fully healed from the experience and was on my way to life with God. Around this time, Atira and I split up for good. It was an amicable decision, and we decided to stay friends and business partners. We also agreed we would be on good terms with each other to set a good example for our son and teach him that hate is not always the way to go when people break up. It was surely a tough time for all of us, but talking again with God, I knew it would pass, and everything would fall into place. It just felt like a change was needed after all we went through over the years; we actually grew closer as friends than we did as a couple.

Around October 2015, I decided to get back into bodybuilding even after a devastating leg injury. For the first time in fourteen years, I was able to grace the stage of a bodybuilding competition. I realized that I had God on my side. Despite going through a horrible accident, I still managed to pull out a victory. It was a very emotional moment as they announced my name as the champion.

I remember being on stage, just looking at the audience, and seeing my son cheering me on and looking so proud. I looked up and thanked God right then and there for saving me. I ended up securing first place in Master Bodybuilding for the category of 40 years and older and came second in open-class bodybuilding for all ages. It truly felt amazing to be able to do what I loved again. From 2015 to 2023, I have competed seven times and feel so utterly blessed and grateful for still being able to do it at almost 50 years old.

Everything was going smoothly, like a stream flowing down the hills, until July 2017, when I received a devastating phone call that would turn my life upside down. Prior to the phone call, I had felt like something was off for a few days. And then, on a cloudy day in July, I got a phone call from my folks informing me that my brother had passed away. Sadly, we had expected this call many times in the past when he was in the prime of his drug addiction. However, he was in a good spot when this happened, so I was understandably confused. *"Why? Why now? Why, when he was doing so well?"* Those questions plagued my mind.

I was told that my brother had had a stroke in bed and passed away from it. The old me would have resorted to drinking and drugs, but that was not an option anymore. I stayed strong for my family, especially for my son, who dearly loved his uncle. In fact, only three weeks away from the bodybuilding competition in 2017, my son said to me, "Dad, why don't you compete in it and dedicate it to uncle?" I asked myself, *"Could I get myself ready that fast?"* Most competitors do a 16-week diet plan leading up to the competition. However, this time, I did it in around 18 days. I had to dedicate my victory to my brother. With the help of God, I am ever so grateful that I got to do that. It was a huge success as I was placed in 2nd position in both categories I competed for. I knew that my brother would be proud, and I knew he was there with me that day.

On a final note, I would ask everyone to reach out to people around them if they need help. Friends or family, never be afraid of opening up before it's too late. If one has no one to reach out to and/or is not confident enough to talk about it, I can tell what they're going through and how it takes people down. People will think you're going crazy when you go through the healing process. Many people thought I was during this process, and I lost a lot of friends when they realized I wasn't the party animal anymore and found God. But do know that positive change only comes from within. So, never let anyone make you feel bad for your healing journey. It's your life, and it's all about you. Own it!

Chapter 13: Dealing With Loss

Life is a journey filled with both joyous moments and challenging obstacles. It is during these difficult times that our determination and eagerness are put to the test. Loss is an inevitable part of the human experience, and its impact can be profound, leaving us in a state of grief and vulnerability. I have explored the journey of dealing with loss and, at the same time, navigated the path toward emotional well-being.

In 2015, after a prolonged absence of about 14 years, I made a triumphant return to bodybuilding by participating in the revered Knight of the Champions Competition. Having recently connected with my spiritual beliefs, this experience became a catalyst for self-discovery and rekindled my passion for body-building, health, and wellness. The stage became a symbol of gratitude, where I could embrace the opportunity to showcase my dedication and resilience despite enduring a severe injury.

Despite the initial skepticism of medical professionals, who believed my leg injury would permanently hinder my ability to train effectively, I persevered. Through determination, discipline, and unwavering faith, I defied everyone's expectations and reclaimed my ability to train my legs with the same intensity as before.

This physical accomplishment stood as a testament to the power of perseverance and indomitable spirit within. Fueled by the momentum gained from the Knight of the Champions competition, I resolved to compete in the 2016 Pro Qualifier, striving to earn my professional bodybuilding card. Although the results of the competition did not align with my expectations, I still maintained a sense of pride in what I brought to the stage.

This setback served as motivation to continue my journey, dedicating myself to ongoing improvement and refining my physique for future endeavors. Undeterred by the outcome, I managed to redouble my efforts, recognizing that true success lies in the continuous pursuit of growth and self-improvement.

****

Strained relationships among siblings can often arise due to various circumstances, and the realm of business is no exception. Initially, my brother and I embarked on a joint business venture with high hopes and shared aspirations. The promise of working together and achieving mutual success fueled our enthusiasm, creating a sense of camaraderie and shared vision.

However, the reality of a failed business began to take its toll on our relationship, causing tension, resentment, and strain. As the business faced challenges, trust began to erode, affecting our ability to communicate effectively and make sound decisions together. The tension between us grew, which extended beyond the business realm and seeped into our personal lives, affecting our interaction and overall well-being.

Taking responsibility for our actions, acknowledging past mistakes, and demonstrating genuine remorse paved the way for healing and renewed understanding. Apart from that, recognizing the need for resolution, my brother and I embarked on a journey to mend our fractured bond. Through dedicated effort and a commitment to reconciliation, we slowly began to rebuild trust and rekindle our connection.

We had established a cherished routine of daily conversations, eagerly anticipating our early morning chats about life and the journey forward. During these heartfelt exchanges, my brother expressed remorse for the past and conveyed his deep gratitude for the restoration of our relationship. Little did I know that my brother's untimely passing in July 2017 would shatter my world so suddenly, leaving a void that could never be filled. Amidst the grief, my heart was burdened with regret as I recalled the days and moments we had wasted, assuming there would always be more time to reconnect and make amends.

In the aftermath of the loss, I found myself haunted by memories of strained moments and unresolved conflicts with my brother. I began to reflect on the preciousness of time and the futility of holding grudges, realizing the significance of addressing issues promptly and cherishing the relationships we hold dear. I yearned for the chance to turn back time, express my love and appreciation, and resolve any lingering disagreements with my brother.

Amidst the regret, I somehow found solace in the fact that I was able to repair our strained relationship with my brother before his passing. I felt a profound sense of gratitude for the moments shared, the apologies exchanged, and the renewed bond we had forged. The experience of loss compelled me to recognize the fleeting nature of life and the importance of seizing opportunities to connect and reconcile.

In my perspective, this serves as a reminder that while the road to repairing strained relationships may be arduous, with determination and perseverance, it is possible to restore them and find renewed strength in the face of adversity.

At the time my brother passed, Atira and I had been separated for two years, with both parties moving on to new romantic involvements. At this point, Atira had found a loving and supportive partner, fostering a harmonious dynamic between them. Her boyfriend was a great guy, and we got along well together. Moreover, he treated my son well, which was all I could ask for, and the two had a great time together, always joking around.

However, the year 2017 proved to be exceptionally challenging for us as we faced consecutive losses. In July, my beloved brother passed away, and just a few months later, in December, Atira's boyfriend unexpectedly departed from this world. I vividly recall the profound shock and dread all of us experienced upon hearing the news, knowing that within a mere span of five months, my 12-year-old son had suffered the loss of two individuals close to his heart.

The sudden and unexpected deaths of two significant figures in my son's life brought overwhelming sadness and confusion. The weight of grief affected his emotional well-being, causing a profound sense of loss and leaving him with a deep longing for the presence of those who had passed.

Coping with the consecutive losses of his uncle and his mother's boyfriend within a short span of time posed a unique challenge for my son. He had to grapple with the complexities of grief, mourning the individuals who held significant roles in his life while also supporting his mother through her own bereavement.

My son and I experienced a range of emotions, including sadness, anger, confusion, and a sense of injustice. However, these emotions intensified as my son struggled to comprehend the finality of death and navigate the absence of those who were once pillars of support and love in his life.

Recognizing the need for stability and support, I put aside my grief and made it a priority to be present for my son during this challenging time. I tried to offer a safe space for him to express his emotions, providing comfort, reassurance, and a listening ear. What I learned from the devastating events of our lives was open and honest conversations about loss and grief play a crucial role in helping children process their emotions.

For many years, I had considered becoming a personal trainer but never really acted on it. Time passed, and the process of healing continued, but the opportunity never presented itself, as I was satisfied with my involvement in the lucrative weed industry. However, after my spiritual awakening, an inner voice urged me to fulfill a greater purpose — that of helping people. The idea of utilizing my body to benefit others resonated deeply within me.

The year 2020, amidst the global pandemic, became a turning point for me. I entered into a new relationship in October 2019, and by the summer of 2020, I had moved in with my girlfriend. During this period, I ventured into personal training with the support of a close high school friend named Lloyd. Lloyd had recently lost 70 pounds and aspired to build muscle.

Utilizing my basement gym, I committed to helping Lloyd achieve his goals by understanding his needs. I was able to design personalized workout programs and meal plans that maximized Lloyd's progress. I recognized the importance of listening to my clients, adapting their strategies, and providing ongoing support to ensure long-term success.

This collaborative effort persisted for a year, resulting in remarkable transformations and heartfelt gratitude from Lloyd. The experience with Lloyd marked a pivotal moment for me. Witnessing the positive impact on his life ignited a newfound passion for helping others. The satisfaction derived from empowering individuals to better themselves mentally and physically became the driving force propelling me forward.

Witnessing the transformation of my clients brought immense joy to my life. Seeing my clients breaking through barriers, surpassing their own expectations, and achieving their goals was incredibly rewarding for me. I understood that their role extended beyond physical training – they were the catalysts for my positive change and personal growth. I experienced the fulfillment that comes from being a part of someone's journey toward self-improvement and embracing a healthier lifestyle.

In the summer of 2019, I fervently prayed for peace after ending a tumultuous relationship. It was during this time that Gina entered my life. I acknowledged the divine intervention and, to this day, express profound gratitude for having found a partner who embodied peace and complimented my journey of growth and service to others.

The year 2021 had also been in my favor as I remarried; my beautiful wife is a real estate professional. Both of us were driven by the shared passion for assisting other people in their respective businesses, finding fulfillment in helping others fulfill their needs.

Chapter 14: Rocky Relationship

There comes a time in our lives when bad things happen one after another, like a string of unfortunate events that just won't stop. It's as if a jinx has been cast upon us, and it feels overwhelming when it seems like bad luck just won't let go. This is a sentiment I know well, as I experienced a series of hardships that left me wondering if there was any end in sight.

It all started with a devastating blow - the loss of my brother. It was a heartache that shook me to my core. Losing a loved one is never easy, and the pain can linger for a long time. And, just when I thought life couldn't get any harder, I found myself entangled in an abusive relationship. The emotional turmoil and hurtful interactions that ensued felt like a continuation of the misfortune that had struck me before.

It's natural for our minds to try to make sense of these patterns, to look for reasons why bad things seem to cluster together. In my case, it began to feel like I was trapped in a cycle of negativity, where every new experience was tinged with the shadow of previous hardships. The weight of this accumulating negativity can be suffocating, making it difficult to see a way out.

As I boarded this new relationship, the raw wounds of my brother's passing were still very much present. The pain of his absence was a constant companion, painting my experiences and interactions. Yet, in the midst of grief's shadow, I found comfort and companionship in the arms of my new girlfriend, Delilah. Little did I know that this relationship would become a source of both comfort and turmoil.

Delilah had a lot of drama in her life, and it affected our relationship. We argued a lot, misunderstood each other, and had many problems. It was like walking a tightrope, trying to handle my own feelings while also dealing with the difficulties in our relationship.

***

It's truly remarkable how children possess an innate ability to sense things beyond what adults may perceive, especially regarding the intentions of people around them. This phenomenon became evident in my own experience. While I was caught up in the complexities of the relationship, my son displayed a keen awareness of Delilah's negative character long before I did.

Children seem to have a sort of "radar" when it comes to understanding people's intentions and emotions. This extraordinary sensitivity to human interactions allows them to form impressions about people, especially those who are close to their parents.

During all the ups and downs, my son became a surprising source of wisdom. He was young, but he could sense that something wasn't right. In the summer of 2019, after a lot of ups and downs, he told me something important. He said, "Dad, I could tell that she was acting strangely, but you didn't want to hear it." His words made me think about things I hadn't wanted to admit.

Looking back, I realized that my son had been quietly struggling. He wanted my attention and time, and he wanted our family to be stable. He saw the problems between me and

Delilah, even though I didn't always see them myself. The arguments we had, especially when she tried to tell me how to be a parent, not only hurt our relationship but also made it hard for me to be a good dad to my son.

This part of my life taught me really important lessons about how love, loss, and family all fit together. It showed me that it's crucial to listen to the people who care about us, even when their opinions are hard to accept.

Now, as I look back on those times, I've learned that the experiences we have, especially the ones that involve loss, shape who we are. And the relationships we build in the present can either fix things, break them, or change us in important ways.

***

I clearly remember a trip that changed everything in my relationship and showed me who Delilah really was. My relationship with her was already in a very tough spot. We often argued, and when alcohol was involved, things got even worse. I had to get a separate hotel room because she was acting crazy.

On that night, things got really out of control. She was drunk and started being mean. I walked down the dark hotel hallway, and she was yelling and hitting me. She hit me and kicked me, and her words hurt even more. She was saying hurtful things that made me feel bad about myself. I was scared to respond because I didn't want things to get worse and for me to get in trouble.

Another time, we were at home and got into a big fight. I was in the bathroom, and she suddenly hit me on the head. I felt the pain, but I didn't do anything back because I worried about making things worse.

All of these fights and hurtful moments added up over time. It got to a point where I couldn't take it anymore. In the summer of 2019, I made a really hard decision. I decided to break up with her. It was like a weight was lifted off my shoulders. I felt so much better without her.

My ex-wife Atira said something that made me think a lot during this time. She asked me, "Who are you?" It made me realize that I had changed because of the bad relationship. I wasn't the strong person she knew me to be. I had let this relationship change me.

After Atira's question, I started to change things. I knew I needed to get back to being myself. Getting out of the abusive relationship was tough, but it was like finding myself again. I had to deal with many difficult things, like how she manipulated me, and I had to remember how to stand up for myself.

Atira's question helped me a lot. It was like a lifeline that pulled me out of a bad situation. It showed me that I needed to change things and get away from the person I had become. It was a hard journey, but I'm glad I went through all of that because I got my life back.

***

Imagine someone saying really mean things to you all the time, like calling you a loser, a terrible person, and a bad father. It hurts a lot when someone talks to you like that, especially when nobody has ever treated you that way before.

I reached a point where I couldn't take it anymore. The hurtful words had worn me down, making me feel really bad about myself. So, I decided to end the relationship. I told her we were breaking up and that she had to leave the house.

She didn't take it well and threatened me. But I didn't back down. I stayed strong and stuck to my decision. It was tough, but I knew I needed to stand up for myself and ensure I was safe.

Breaking up with her and standing my ground was a big step toward getting my life back. It wasn't easy, especially after enduring so much. But I knew I deserved better and had to protect myself from that kind of treatment.

There are moments when we feel really sad in our lives, and it seems like everything is gone. But even in these tough times, something good can happen. This happened to me, too, reminding me that even when things are very dark, there can be a little bit of hope.

After a brutal breakup, I felt really vulnerable and lost. The relationship had hurt me a lot, and I didn't feel good about myself anymore. I could understand what Austin Powers meant when he talked about losing his "mojo." It was like a part of me was missing, and I felt confused and sad.

When things were tough, I turned to something that makes me feel better, even if I can't explain it: prayer. I asked God for comfort, peace, and a little light to help me through the hard times. I also asked for someone to be with, a partner to share my life with and make me feel better.

While it's natural to feel like we're under a jinx when things go wrong, it's essential to remember that we have the power to shift our narrative. We can choose to break free from the cycle of misfortune by seeking positive relationships and making choices that align with our values and aspirations. It might take time, but with determination and support, we can rewrite our story and create a future that is not defined by past hardships.

Life is full of surprises, and we don't always know what will happen next. I didn't know that the answer to my prayers would come from meeting someone unexpected at a sushi restaurant nearby. The waitress there turned out to be someone I wasn't looking for but needed. My story is about believing in something bigger than us, finding unexpected connections, and knowing that there's a bigger plan even when things hurt.

Chapter 15: More Troubles in 2019

Life is a journey filled with happiness, sorrows, and ups and downs. We all know it is full of unexpected twists and turns that can take us by surprise at any moment. When we think we have everything figured out, something unexpected happens that challenges our plans and forces us to adapt. While often daunting, these surprises can lead to new opportunities and growth.

The unpredictability of life teaches us to be flexible and tough, and we learn to navigate through the highs and lows with grace and courage. It reminds us that change is inevitable and that we can't always control what happens to us but can control how we respond.

When we embrace the unexpected, it can open doors to new experiences, relationships, and perspectives that we may never have encountered otherwise. It encourages us to step out of our comfort zones, explore new possibilities, and discover hidden strengths within ourselves.

While it can be unsettling to face the unknown, it's also what makes life exciting and dynamic. Welcoming the unpredictability of life allows us to live more fully. We learn to appreciate the expedition and cherish the moments of surprise, wonder, and growth along the way.

Sometimes, we don't understand that certain problems are sent toward us to make us stronger; something similar happened to me. I had not even completely recovered from the trauma of my broken relationship when I was struck by another tragedy in the same year. I had no time to heal or recover as the problems came one after another without a breather. What I did not understand at that point was how this issue was sent my way for my betterment.

It was in 2019 that a devastating fire broke out at a large shop located at the rear of a secluded acreage property. This facility was specifically built for the production of marijuana. While I did not own the property myself, I was deeply involved in it through a business partnership with the owner.

If I talk about the timing of this incident, it could not have been worse for me personally. As I mentioned earlier, it was around the same period when I had just ended the relationship with Delilah. This further added a lot of emotional strain to an already challenging situation. The news of the fire reached me while I was at home, triggering a sense of déjà vu. I could not shake the memory of a similar incident about a decade earlier when I received an urgent call about a fire on Christmas Eve.

This particular venture had always been an uphill battle for me since the beginning. Numerous individuals had invested their money with high hopes of seeing a profitable return on their investment. However, the progress was quite slow, and some stakeholders' frustrations grew. Many investors became increasingly resentful due to the prolonged time it was taking to realize any financial gains from the project.

With the fire outbreak, my initial sinking feeling was replaced by a growing sense of dread. I knew that this incident would undoubtedly lead to a significant loss for everyone involved in it in one way or another. The investors, who were already frustrated by the delays, would now face the harsh reality of losing their investment entirely. I was worried that the financial setback would likely fuel their anger and disappointment and make the situation even more challenging to navigate.

The fire destroyed the physical infrastructure and shattered the hopes and dreams of those who had put their trust and money into the project. It was a stark reminder of the unpredictable nature of business and the risks associated with investment. As I reflected on the situation, I could not help but feel a profound sense of responsibility for the outcome. I was concerned about the impact it would have on the lives of the investors and stakeholders.

When the matter was investigated, the cause of the fire was traced back to the generator used to power the marijuana production operation. The incident was so significant that it made the front page of the local newspaper the following week. Seeing the shop engulfed in flames on the front page was surreal. Despite the stress and tests that followed, I felt a sense of relief on a personal level.

It was undeniably tough to deal with the aftermath of such a devastating event, especially with the loss of investment and unhappy investors. However, since I knew that this was the last illegal marijuana factory that I would ever be involved with brought a weight off my shoulders. The entire experience served as a turning point in my life, as it marked the end of a chapter filled with challenges and risks.

If something like this had happened in the past, facing such adversity might have led me down a destructive path. I would have definitely turned to alcohol and drugs as coping mechanisms; however, this time was different. Instead of avoiding the situation or numbing the pain through substance abuse, I confronted it head-on. I did not run away from the situation and made sure to help those affected. I took the necessary steps to address the fire's aftermath and worked toward finding a resolution for the investors and stakeholders affected by the loss.

While the financial impact of the fire was significant, the experience positively impacted me spiritually. It allowed me to let go of the negativity and stress associated with the job. I realized that facing setbacks and difficulties can sometimes lead to personal growth and a deeper understanding of oneself.

My life did not stop at any point, and I continued to move forward despite my hardships. The fire served as a poignant reminder of the impermanence of material possessions and the importance of resilience in the face of misfortune. It taught me valuable lessons about accountability and the importance of adapting to change.

Whenever I look back, I realize that regardless of how painful the experience was, it helped shape me into a stronger and sturdier individual. It served as a catalyst for personal growth and pushed me to confront my trials head-on and find healthier ways to cope with adversity.

After the tumultuous period following the fire and the breakup, I found myself seeking a new direction in life. I had been on a spiritual journey and felt a growing desire to impact and help others positively. While the path was not clear at first, I had a strong intuition that I was meant to assist people in some meaningful way.

Just when I was trying to figure out how to do it, a few months later, an unexpected opportunity presented itself when an old friend reached out to me. We had not seen each other in years, but he wanted to get in shape and asked for my guidance. This unexpected connection sparked an idea that eventually led me to become a personal trainer. It felt like the universe was aligning things in a way that allowed me to combine my newfound passion for helping others with a practical and fulfilling career.

Another valuable thing that happened during this period was that my focus shifted toward finding peace and spending quality time with my son. The breakup prompted me to seek solace in solitude, so I spent my time reflecting on my life and praying for a rightful direction. My prayers centered on finding inner peace and becoming the best father I could be for my son, especially as he entered his teenage years. I knew it was the time when he would need me the most.

My son and I began to bond over our shared love for sushi, and making regular visits to Sushi Palace became a cherished tradition. I started to enjoy our time together and realized how important it was to spend time with him. It was not only my son who needed me, but I also desperately needed his company.

I distinctly remember that on one of these outings, I was captivated by the beauty of one of the servers. My attention was so fixed on her that my son jokingly pointed out my distraction and reminded me to focus on our time together. We laughed it off, but little did I know that this chance encounter would bring the peace and happiness I had been seeking for a long time.

As I got to know the gorgeous waitress better, I found out her name was Gina. With time, we formed a connection beyond mere attraction. She became a source of comfort and stability during the transition and uncertainty in my life. Her presence brought a sense of calmness and contentment and filled the void that had been left behind by the sufferings I had faced in my life.

Her companionship helped me rediscover the joy in simple moments and appreciate the beauty of new beginnings. Our relationship blossomed, and she played a significant role in helping me heal and move forward from the hardships I had experienced.

Looking back, it's clear that each challenge and setback I faced led me closer to where I am today. The fire, the breakup, and the following struggles were pivotal moments that shaped my journey. They made me discover my passion for helping others and finding peace in unexpected places.

As I embraced this new chapter in my life, I comprehended that true fulfillment comes from embracing change, seeking growth, and finding strength in vulnerability. My experiences taught me the importance of resilience, gratitude, and the transformative power of love and connection. The twists and turns of my journey took me to a place of healing, purpose, and happiness.

I learned to trust the process, embrace the unknown, and appreciate the people and experiences enriching our lives. They made me realize how ungrateful we could become sometimes and taught me to be more thankful. I made peace with the fact that everything in life happens for a reason that is certainly in our best interest.

Chapter 16: More Loss

2019 was a year of intense experiences that life threw at me. Without a doubt, I had a very eventful year, with some people leaving and others entering my life. Four main events took place in that year that are worth highlighting. Firstly, I navigated the tumultuous waters of ending a two-year relationship, which shattered me. It was a journey fraught with emotional ups and downs.

Amidst this personal turmoil, I found solace and distraction in an unexpected arena: the world of bodybuilding. Despite the emotional strain I was going through, I gathered the strength to compete in a bodybuilding contest. I was determined to put all my energy into pursuing my newfound passion.

However, even as I chased physical excellence, life delivered another blow with the loss of a cherished friend. He was someone who has had a constant presence in my life. He was like a brother to me and a very close confidant. He was not just my buddy but shared a close brotherly bond with me. The grief of this loss undoubtedly weighed heavily on my heart and cast a shadow over even the best of times.

Yet, amid the turbulence, a ray of light emerged as I crossed paths with someone who changed the course of my life: my future wife, Gina. As soon as I met her, a new chapter filled with hope, love, and the promise of a brighter tomorrow began.

The period leading up to my bodybuilding competition in the wake of a breakup was undeniably challenging. With just ten days to go until the big event, I was steering through two life-altering events. It was challenging to deal with the emotional wreckage of ending a big relationship while simultaneously getting ready for one of the most crucial events in my fitness journey. The added stress could have easily derailed my focus, but I remained firm regardless of the weight of emotions that bore down on me.

I distinctly remember that the closer the competition got, the more pressure there was, especially in that critical last week called "peak week." This was the end of sixteen weeks of intense training and disciplined dieting, during which every little thing counted. The ideal use of this time would have been fine-tuning my physical and mental preparation without outside pressures. However, the reality was far from ideal as I grappled with the breakup's aftermath.

Prayer became a source of comfort and strength for me during this turbulent time. I prayed to God for direction and asked for the mental clarity and fortitude required to face the difficulties head-on. My prayers were miraculously answered and gave me the strength and determination needed to complete the task.

Fortunately, I put on a fantastic performance on stage despite the extra weight of emotional upheaval. I performed above and beyond expectations and secured second place in all three categories I competed in. I vividly recall how I felt an indescribable sense of fulfillment and success at that moment. It was evidence of my unshakeable commitment, tenacity, and capacity to flourish in the face of adversity.

Looking back, I realize that emotional and mental toughness were just as important as physical ability in getting to the competition podium. It served as a reminder that, even in the most difficult circumstances, greatness can be attained, and trials can be overcome with perseverance and faith.

After having a contest, I went on vacation with my son to have some fun and feel a little better. I remember the sweltering heat of the summer day that seemed to intensify the weight of the news, which altered my world forever. My son and I went inside to the kitchen table to find comfort and nourishment as we escaped the scorching sun. I had no idea I would receive a phone call that would rock me to my very core and shatter that brief window of relief we were enjoying.

As my phone rang, it displayed the number of my best friend Dick's sister, Eileen. I felt a wave of dread come over me at that very moment. I had a gut feeling that there was a problem and that she would give me some bad news. I picked it up with a pounding heart and prepared for the news that would arrive shortly. The news that Eileen had to break to me was beyond heartbreaking: Dick, my brother and lifelong friend, had died unexpectedly. I was left reeling with shock and grief as the weight of her words struck me and made everything stop.

My son was acutely aware of the seriousness of the situation and the gloomy atmosphere permeating the room. He could easily guess by the look on my face that something horrible had happened. His naive gaze reflected my shock and anguish as I tried to process the unexpected death of someone so close to my heart. I broke the terrible news to him with a heavy heart. I was crying as I tried to process how big of a loss this was for both of us.

My son's poignant question cut through the silence in the middle of sorrow, echoing the anguish and confusion that tore my soul. His voice quivered with emotion as he questioned, "Dad, why does this keep happening?" The question struck a deep chord, serving as a sobering reminder of the incomprehensible mysteries of life and death that even adults find difficult to fathom.

I relied on my faith for comfort during the pain and uncertainty because I believed that a higher power had a purpose. No matter how unbelievable it may have seemed in the wake of such a significant loss, I decided to be patient. My mind was filled with flashbacks of my recent times with Dick which provided a momentary relief amidst the suffering. A few weeks earlier, he came to my bodybuilding competition to support me, demonstrating our strong friendship, which we had endured over time.

When I reflected on the precious time we had shared, I was grateful for the unexpected opportunity I had recently gotten to reconnect with him. It was now bittersweet to think back on our last night together; it was a long-overdue guys' night full of jokes and companionship. I had no idea it would be my last chance to see him, which served as a sobering reminder of how fleeting life is and how important it is to savor each moment.

As I grappled with the pain of loss, I held onto the memories of my dear friend and found solace in the knowledge that his spirit would live on. I will always cherish his beautiful memories and treasure the indelible mark he left on my heart.

As a beautiful tribute to Dick's memory, I decided to adopt his beloved Rottweiler puppy after his passing. Since I knew how much he adored the furry companion, I wanted to ensure she would continue receiving the love and care she deserved. I wanted to keep a part of Dick's spirit alive through her presence, so I took her home with me. It was a gesture filled with love and compassion, honoring the special bond Dick shared with his canine companion.

After experiencing his untimely death, I gained a profound appreciation for the importance of living in the present and cherishing the relationships that enrich our lives. Losing him suddenly made me appreciate life more and urged me to embrace each moment. I learned to value the connections that brought joy and meaning to my existence.

In moments of reflection and prayer, I sought solace and comfort for Dick and trusted God to grant him eternal peace and rest. In the midst of the sorrow of loss, prayer provided me comfort and consolation. I realized that we should never take any moment for granted as it could be our end, or someone dear to us might breathe their last.

The wave of loss that swept through my life during that period left me contemplating the very essence of existence. With the passing of my brother-like best friend, whom my son affectionately referred to as "uncle," I was confronted with the fragility of life in its rawest form.

Amidst the sadness and suffering, I grappled with profound questions about mortality and the purpose of our journey in this world. However, despite this existential turmoil, I gained a fresh perspective on life's small pleasures. I began to be thankful for the feel of the sun on my face, the laughter shared with loved ones, and the gentle breeze rustling through the trees.

Even though my heart was heavy, I found strength in the need to support my son—who, at such a young age, was also navigating the rough seas of loss. I found resiliency and purpose in being a parent and used my own sorrow to provide stability and solace for my child. It was proof of the unbreakable bond between a parent and their child and a glimmer of hope amid despair.

I overcame everything and came out stronger and more resilient as a deep sense of gratitude drove me for every day I got to wake up. I considered myself fortunate to be able to see a brand-new dawn. I cherished the gift of life and the enduring power of love to sustain us through even the darkest of times. I found comfort in the priceless moments spent with loved ones in the face of loss.

Chapter 17: A New Hope

I think that getting out of tough circumstances can occasionally be likened to attempting to navigate a maze without a way out. Even in the face of hardship, there is a glimmer of hope that shows the path to a brighter tomorrow. This journey is marked by strength, perseverance, and an unwavering faith in the possibility of renewal.

One of the best things about humans is that we never give up easily. That fighting spirit helps us conquer challenges. Though hopelessness is a heavy burden, everyone can rise above the darkness and welcome the light. This capacity to recover serves as a guiding light, inspiring people to press on in the face of uncertainty or danger.

Furthermore, overcoming adversity promotes a deep sense of self-discovery. In chaotic situations, people often find hidden strengths and abilities they never knew they had. Through introspection and self-reflection, they begin to re-evaluate who they are and what their purpose in life is. As a result, they gain a fresh resilience that enables them to face life's challenges head-on.

Maybe the most transformative aspect of the experience is the new perspective that comes from overcoming adversity. People emerge from the depths of despair with a renewed sense of clarity and purpose. They no longer regard obstacles as insurmountable barriers but rather as opportunities for growth and change.

When people go through difficult times, they feel that they are more deeply connected to each other than before. They realize the importance of being associated with a community and the powerful impact of kindness and sympathy. They find peace in knowing that they are not alone in their battles and that they can overcome even the toughest of battles by supporting each other. In my opinion, emerging from difficult times is not merely about surviving, but it's also about fighting back.

While dealing with life's uncertain nature, many people resort to prayer as a source of comfort. They believe that reaching out to the divine power can bring about the answers and guidance they seek. This is true in a lot of people's cases, including my own, as I reflect on a pivotal moment in the summer of 2019.

I was in a horrible mental and emotional state after going through a troublesome breakup. My broken soul yearned for peace as I was at my lowest. It was during this time of contemplation and seeking that I turned to prayer, fervently asking for the serenity to help me get through this heartbreaking situation.

A few months passed, and even though the pain of losing my ex-girlfriend remained, I held onto the belief that my prayers would be answered in due time. Little did I know that the universe had already begun to work things in my favor. I had no clue that out of nowhere, it would have me end up at a place called Sushi Palace.

I distinctly remember that it was a warm summer evening when Gina first caught my eye. She was certainly an epitome of perfection and grace amid the noise and chaos of the restaurant.

There was an unavoidable attraction that drew my attention toward her. It was something beyond the physical allure that ignited a spark of curiosity within me.

I began to visit the restaurant more often, not just for the delicious food but also for a chance to stare at my beautiful future wife. Even though she used to have an extremely tight schedule, we still shared fleeting moments of connection. We would pass smiles at each other that would always leave us wanting for more.

As the days turned into weeks and then months, my admiration for Gina continued to grow, yet I hesitated to act on my burgeoning feelings. Fear of rejection and uncertainty held me back until one fateful day when I mustered the courage to speak my truth.

I have a vivid recollection of the day when I finally decided to compliment Gina on her hair. I did it while settling my bill at the restaurant with trembling hands. I did not know that a small gesture like this would change the course of my life forever. She responded with a radiant smile and a gracious "thank you," which emboldened me to take a leap of faith and ask her out on a date.

I could feel the tension building as I waited for her answer, my heart pounding with equal parts nervousness and excitement. Then, like a soft murmur in the night, my phone buzzed to let me know that Gina had sent me a message to confirm our first date.

Our feelings for each other started to blossom, just like something magical in a storybook. We found out that our birthdays were only one day apart—a coincidental fact that seemed to be fate nudging us in the right direction. Soon after that, we went on a vacation with an exciting journey ahead of us, ready to be filled in with the colors of our recently discovered love.

With each passing day, my affection for Gina deepened, as did my gratitude for the answered prayers that led me to her. What began as a simple plea for peace blossomed into a love story for the ages. It was a testament to the power of faith, fate, and the firm belief that love always finds a way.

Even after all these years, I found myself continually amazed by the incredible person Gina is. We started our journey with guarded hearts because we had both gone through difficult breakups at that time. But when we opened up and let down our barriers, love blossomed between us. Now, when we reflect on our past, we are frequently amazed at how random our love story was.

Gina, who was originally from Korea, was traveling the world on a work visa to Canada with the intention of going to South America later. But something called fate, or some higher power, moved to unite two people who lived on opposite sides of the planet and were 19 years apart.

Even though our backgrounds and upbringings were completely different, we found peace and comfort in each other's company. I had not felt this kind of calm in my life since I was a young child, but Gina gave it to me. Her presence acted as a soothing salve that mended the scars left by previous disappointments and uncertainties.

The thing that really got to me was how well Gina fit into my life. My son, being as sensitive as ever, recognized right away how much she loved me and gave her a big hug. His warmth and acceptance of Gina said volumes about the sincerity of our relationship.

Even my ex-wife, Atira, surprised me with her reaction to Gina. Instead of resentment or jealousy, she greeted Gina with a punch on the shoulder and words of encouragement. Her approval echoed what everyone else seemed to feel – that Gina was truly one of the good ones, and I shouldn't let her slip away.

Our love story is proof of life's unpredictability and the ability of love to overcome obstacles like age, distance, and cultural differences. It serves as a reminder that sometimes, the deepest connections come from the most unlikely encounters.

Gina and I are so happy we became friends. We're really enjoying this time together! Being with her makes me feel happier and more fulfilled than ever. It feels like our love was meant to be, not just chance. I know for a fact that it will lead us to a future full of love, joy, and limitless opportunities, just like it has until now.

It was in 2021, when the pandemic had become extremely challenging for everyone, that Gina and I decided to tie the knot. It was not at all like the wedding day we had imagined. Only ten people were able to physically attend our ceremony due to COVID restrictions. It was quite disheartening to know that Gina's parents could not be present in person because of travel limitations. So, they joined us virtually via Zoom from Korea on our big day and made it a bittersweet moment.

I remember a lot of people questioned our choice to go ahead with the wedding in the given circumstances. They inquired whether we ought to hold off until things calmed down and more people could come. However, waiting any further was not an option for us. Pandemic or not, we were prepared to make the big step into married life and start our forever together.

The constraints during that time were strict, as nobody was allowed to have any gatherings or parties. There was a rule about only having ten guests at formal events, but I'm not very good at following rules. So, after exchanging vows in an intimate ceremony, we decided to throw caution to the wind and host a reception at our house. We did not care about the repercussions that it could have.

Our house turned into a center of joy, love, and laughter. It was a magnificent evening full of dancing, music, and meaningful conversations with different people. Everyone was ecstatic to be able to socialize and catch up with loved ones after months of lockdown, despite the circumstances.

We started out planning for only ten people, but by the evening, there were way more! Since everyone we had invited was desperate for human interaction, so all our friends and family flocked to our house. They transformed our little get-together into a bustling event. It demonstrated the human spirit's persistence because, in spite of hardship, we were able to find happiness and companionship.

There was an electrifying vibe throughout, with smiles beaming from every corner and laughter resonating through the hallways of our home. As Gina and I moved through the crowd, we took in all of our guests' warmth and love. It was a celebration of friendship, family, and the victory of love over hard times in addition to our union.

In retrospect, our COVID wedding served as a monument to the ability of love to overcome all challenges. We persevered, determined to start our journey as husband and wife with our loved ones by our sides, regardless of the obstacles and constraints.

We were left with hearts full of gratitude and lifelong memories as the evening drew to an end and our guests said goodbye. Our wedding day may not have been what we originally imagined, but it was perfect in its own unique way. It was a symbol of love's ability to triumph over everything and bring people together, no matter what.

Chapter 18: Moving Forward With God

Finding faith has really helped me understand why I'm in this world and what matters in life. It's like having a steady source of direction, consolation, and encouragement regardless of the difficulties we encounter.

Above all, having a relationship with God gives us direction. The idea that there is a higher power that genuinely loves us and has a purpose for our lives is comforting. This conviction can give us the bravery to face any uncertainty and the tenacity to get past challenges.

Furthermore, having a relationship with God provides a deep sense of assurance and serenity. Knowing that God is always there to hear our prayers and that we are not alone can be immensely reassuring, especially in times of hardship. It's similar to having a friend who is constantly ready to lend ears, provide encouragement, and give advice.

Being close to God can help us figure out who we are supposed to be and what we're here to do. We can discover our true selves and our special talents and passions through prayer, meditation, and introspection. This self-awareness can guide us in making decisions that align with our values and aspirations.

Furthermore, a strong relationship with God can help us feel more connected to other people and the outside world. It is easier to sympathize with others' struggles and celebrate their victories when we acknowledge the divine essence in each other and ourselves. In my opinion, we can create a more loving and peaceful community through acts of kindness, compassion, and service motivated by this sense of interconnectedness.

I believe faith in God can provide a source of hope and resilience in the face of adversity. Believing that God works all things together for good can give us the strength to persevere through difficult times and to trust that better days are ahead. Even when things get tough, this hope keeps us going. It helps us see that challenges can make us stronger and even better.

Life has shown me that a close relationship with God can bring gratitude and joy into our daily lives. We are overcome with a deep sense of gratitude for the Creator, who made all of this possible. We can never fully thank God for all the blessings in our lives, from the beauty of the natural world to the affection of family and friends. We can feel more satisfied and fulfilled when we adopt a grateful mindset and shift our focus from what we lack to what we have.

Being close to God is beneficial for you in many ways. Faith can improve every aspect of our lives, from offering consolation and direction to encouraging thankfulness and a sense of purpose. Therefore, remember that God is always present and waiting to embrace you with open arms. So, whether we are having trouble making a decision, experiencing uncertainty, or just wanting to have a closer relationship with the divine, we should never delay it.

My life took a significant turn when I came home to God. Even though I continued to experience difficulties and setbacks, my growing faith changed how I handled them. Rather than turning to harmful coping mechanisms like drugs and alcohol, my relationship with God gave me resilience and strength.

How I handled adversity was one of the biggest shifts I went through. With God by my side, I no longer felt overpowered or defenseless in difficult situations. Rather, realizing that I wasn't the only one going through tough times gave me a strong sense of inner confidence and serenity.

My mornings became a special time to be thankful and reflect. Every day, I set aside some time to express my thankfulness for all the blessings in my life before the daily grind took over. I became aware of how much I had to be thankful for, from being healthy and eating a balanced diet to having loving family and friends.

The biggest thing that struck me was the change in perspective. Things that I once took for granted became sources of immense gratitude and joy. A warm meal, a roof over my head, and the laughter of loved ones are examples of the small blisses in life that make me feel deeply grateful.

Furthermore, I felt that I had direction and a purpose because of my relationship with God. Knowing that I was loved without condition by a higher power gave me the confidence to go after my goals and take on life's obstacles without any fear. I had a sense of clarity and purpose that led me forward as I no longer felt lost or aimless.

The way I was able to find calm in the midst of chaos was maybe the most amazing change I have ever been through in my entire life. I had a deep sense of serenity and faith in God's plan despite the loss and uncertainty. I no longer felt the need to stray from the right path and get involved in harmful things. I found comfort in prayer and meditation as I knew that God was always with me.

I can safely say that coming home to God changed everything for the better. It gave me strength where there was weakness, hope where there was despair, and gratitude where there was once indifference. I found a new way of living through faith– one filled with purpose, peace, and profound joy.

I had a renewed sense of purpose and a desire to have a positive influence on others when I came to know God. It seemed as though doors of opportunity were opening for me with relative ease. One such opportunity came unexpectedly when an old high school friend, Lloyd, reached out to me on Facebook.

Lloyd's message came as a surprise, but it also felt like a sign from above. He expressed his desire to start working out and getting in shape, acknowledging his struggle with being extremely overweight. When I first saw him, I was taken aback by how much he had changed since high school. I could not help but ask, "Lloyd, is that you?"

Having worked out and competed in bodybuilding competitions for more than 30 years, I knew I had the knowledge and abilities to assist Lloyd in transforming his life. We set out on a quest for improved fitness and health with persistence and devotion. Lloyd was firm in his commitment to change, even though it was not easy.

Together, we created a customized exercise and diet plan that suited his needs and set reasonable goals. Lloyd pushed himself to the limit every week, losing weight and building muscle. Seeing the transformation happen right in front of my eyes was amazing.

In the span of a year, Lloyd lost an astonishing 70 pounds, and his progress did not stop there. We continued to work together, improving his body and overall fitness level. The change in him was nothing short of remarkable, and to this day, he maintains an impressive physique. Ever since that time, he has had a newfound sense of confidence that has become a part of his personality.

Lloyd's transformation was a decisive moment for me – it was like a lightbulb had gone off in my head. I came to understand that I had the ability to assist people in improving not just their physical condition but also their mental and emotional well-being. Lloyd's victory really motivated me, so I decided to follow my fitness passion and get my personal training certification.

After learning and growing from my own experiences and travels, I decided to use what I gained to help others. I began by announcing that I was accepting new clients. Before I knew it, my calendar was full of people who were ready to change their physical appearance and enhance their general health.

Being a personal trainer has been tremendously fulfilling. Nothing compares to the satisfaction of seeing someone reach their objectives and experience the positive effects it has on their lives. Every success story I hear about, whether it's about someone getting stronger, losing weight, or just feeling more comfortable in their skin, makes me believe even more in the ability to help others.

My job is not just about physical transformations. What I enjoy most about my job is the chance to empower people to take charge of their health and make positive changes that go far beyond the gym. It's about helping people reach their greatest potential, developing resilience, and instilling confidence.

To put it precisely, my journey from accepting God into my life to becoming a personal trainer is evidence of the overpowering influence that one person can have on the lives of others. I have practically witnessed and experienced the transformational power of faith. I have found fulfillment, purpose, and a deep sense of joy through helping others, and these things continue to inspire me every day.

I hope this book serves as a ray of hope for those who feel lost in the darkness, weighed down by despair. I have been there myself, hovering on the edge of destruction, but God's love and grace pulled me back from the brink. Without Him, I would not be here today.

I used to be on a destructive path, surrounded by obscurity and hopelessness. But God, in His boundless mercy, greeted me with a warm embrace and pointed out the path to return to the light. Although the journey was not simple, nonetheless, it was worthwhile.

Once you have found the light, the important thing is to follow it and stick to it. Even though I was as far from God as one could be, His love knows no limits. There is always hope, no matter how far gone you may feel.

If you find yourself drowning in despair, seek change. Pray for it, believe in it, and be open to the unexpected blessings that come your way. You may be surprised by the transformation that takes place within you and the newfound sense of purpose and peace that accompanies it.